Raising an American Girl

Parenting Advice
for the Real World

★ American Girl®

A Letter from the President of American Girl

Dear Parents,
One of the things I like best about my job is that I get to connect with girls and families who've made this company a part of their lives. I love reading the letters that girls and parents write us or, better yet, actually talking to them in our stores and cafes, and even on the phones. (All American Girl employees take orders during the busy holiday season.)

Girls' smiles and their parents' heartfelt words remind me again and again that we are so much more than a doll company. We are a "girl company" dedicated to being on your side—the side of adults who want their girls to grow up to be the very best they can be.

In this spirit of partnership, I am proud to introduce our parenting book *Raising an American Girl*—a collection of wise, inspiring messages from American Girl's own "dream team."

Our Experts
The authors of these essays are the experts we turn to in creating our books and *American Girl* magazine. They are the people who best know the hearts and minds of girls; they are educators, psychologists, physicians, and counselors, many of whom are parents of girls. These folks keep us grounded in the realities of raising girls today. They remind us that many caring conversations with our daughters can be much more powerful than One Big Talk.

A Book for Busy Parents
Our hope is that reading this book will be like having your own series of short chats with our thoughtful advisors. You'll see that topics are covered in a way that's easy to digest, with "big truths" and short, insightful essays from experts. Every essay is accompanied by "Try This" ideas—activities and conversation starters designed to provide moments of connection between girls and their parents. Many of these were written by Amy Lynch, an author long devoted to nurturing meaningful communication between girls, mothers, and fathers.

Flip through the pages and look for what speaks to you. There's no "right" order in which to read this book, just as there's no single right way to parent.

Why Now?

This book comes to you at a time of unprecedented change for girls. There's a real struggle today between popular culture and the many parents who find themselves on the defensive. It can be hard even to find a television show you can comfortably watch with your daughter. Add to this the Internet, which provides your daughter with easy access to millions of photos, videos, and audio clips every day.

Parents feel overwhelmed, and we understand that. What I like best about this book is that its positive tone reminds us how, as parents, we can—and do—make a difference. It reminds us of the simple joy of a conversation in the car on the way to school or the power of a talk in the kitchen while soup simmers on the stove.

In the end, you're the expert. You know your daughter better than anyone. In the words of one of our authors: "Each day, our daughters are becoming. Our role—and it is a sacred one—is to guide, observe, and celebrate." And each time you open the pages of this book, you do all that. You're there for her.

So, thank you for allowing American Girl to share in this moment in your lives. I'm glad we can be partners on this journey.

Sincerely,

Ellen L. Brothers

Ellen L. Brothers
President
American Girl

Contributing Authors

Dr. Evelyn Bassoff is a clinical psychologist, an artist, and a writer. She is the author of many journal articles and books, including *Mothering Ourselves: Help and Healing for Adult Daughters* and *Cherishing Our Daughters: How Parents Can Raise Girls to Become Confident Women.*

Formerly an adjoint associate professor at the University of Colorado and a columnist for *Parents* magazine, Dr. Bassoff is in private practice in Boulder, Colorado, where she lives with her husband. Her close-knit family includes two adult children and their families and several "adopted" Sudanese adults and their children.

For the past seven years, the Bassoffs have helped young refugees from war-torn southern Sudan make homes in Boulder and get college educations. She helped launch the nonprofit CSAW, the Community of Sudanese and American Women and Men.

Virginia Beane Rutter, MS in clinical counseling, is a licensed marriage and family therapist and author of two books on raising girls. *Embracing Persephone: How to Be the Mother You Want for the Daughter You Cherish* uses interviews with women and girls to encourage awareness in a mother's responses to her adolescent girl and to uncover the archetype at work beneath these difficult teenage years. *Celebrating Girls: Nurturing and Empowering Our Daughters* offers hands-on suggestions for raising daughters from birth to adolescence, with an attitude of valuing the feminine and of honoring the deeper meaning of everyday rituals.

Ms. Beane Rutter is a certified analytical psychologist, a member of and on the teaching faculty of the C. G. Jung Institute in San Francisco. She has a private practice in Mill Valley, California. She is also the mother of a son and a daughter, who often help her edit her writing.

Dr. Roni Cohen-Sandler's first book, *"I'm Not Mad, I Just Hate You!": A New Understanding of Mother-Daughter Conflict*, was a national bestseller. Her second book, *"Trust Me, Mom—Everyone Else Is Going!"* won a National Parenting Publication Award gold medal. Her most recent book, *Stressed-Out Girls: Helping Them Thrive in the Age of Pressure* is based on a national study of 3,000 teens and preteens and describes the pressures girls today are experiencing in their efforts to be successful—as well as what parents and educators can do to help them.

Dr. Cohen-Sandler speaks throughout the country and abroad to schools, community organizations, hospitals, and corporations. She also consults for television and is a frequent guest on national programs, including *Oprah*, *The Today Show*, *Good Morning America*, and *The Early Show*. Her expert opinions have appeared in numerous newspapers and national magazines. Dr. Cohen-Sandler is married, with a daughter and a son in their twenties.

Patti Kelley Criswell, MSW, is a clinical social worker and has been in private practice for 15 years. Criswell is the author of a number of American Girl advice books for young readers, including *Stand Up for Yourself & Your Friends*, *A Smart Girl's Guide to Friendship Troubles*, *Go For It*, and *Friends: Making Them and Keeping Them*.

Ms. Criswell specializes in working with girls, young women, and their families. She is an adjunct professor of social work at Western Michigan University and writes and speaks nationally on the topics of girl aggression and body image. She is married and is the mother of two children, who have been her greatest joy and inspiration. She lives near Kalamazoo, Michigan.

Dr. JoAnn Deak has spent more than 20 years as an educator and psychologist, helping children develop into confident and competent adults. The latter half of that period has focused on working with parents and teachers in their roles as guides for children. A quote on her Web site best describes her perspective: "Every interaction a child has, during the course of a day, influences the adult that child will become."

Dr. Deak is the founder of The DEAK Group, a consulting service for schools and parents. She specializes in demystifying complex issues of child development, learning, identity formation, and brain research. She has been an advisor to Outward Bound and a past chair of the National Committee for Girls and Women in Independent Schools. She is the author of numerous magazine articles and books, including *Girls Will Be Girls: Raising Confident and Courageous Daughters* and her current work in progress, *The Brain Matters: A Middle of the Road Guide for Parenting and Teaching.*

Amy Lynch has spent many years delving into the lives and communication styles of girls, young adults, and their families. A writer, keynote speaker, and moderator of numerous national workshops, she authored the American Girl books *A Smart Girl's Guide to Her Family*, for young readers, and *"How Can You Say That?": What to Say to Your Daughter When One of You Just Said Something Awful*, for parents. Ms. Lynch also founded *Daughters* newsletter for the parents of adolescent girls. Her ideas about how girls grow strong have been featured in publications including the *Washington Post, USA Today, Utne Reader,* and *Good Housekeeping.*

When she is not writing about parenting girls, Ms. Lynch writes, consults, and speaks about young people in the workplace through her company, Bottom Line Conversations. Her daughters are Sara, now 22, and Jean, 20, to whom she dedicates her work on this book.

Dr. Lynda Madison is a licensed psychologist and an associate professor in pediatrics and psychiatry at Creighton University School of Medicine and director of FOCCUS, Inc. USA, which offers training and research on marriage and family relationships. Dr. Madison previously directed behavioral health services at Children's Hospital in Omaha, Nebraska, for 22 years.

Dr. Madison is the author of several American Girl books for young readers, including *Food & You, The Feelings Book*, and *The Feelings Book Journal*. She is the author of *Parenting with Purpose: Progressive Discipline from Birth to Four* and *Keep Talking: A Mother-Daughter Guide to the Preteen Years*. She has shared her expertise on many national radio and television programs, including *The Today Show,* and on MSNBC.

Dr. Madison seeks to promote commitment, respect, and trustworthiness in all relationships and provides workshops internationally for parents, health professionals, corporations, schools, and other organizations. She is married and has two young adult daughters.

Dr. Lynn Ponton is a professor of psychiatry at the University of California, San Francisco, and a practicing psychiatrist and psychoanalyst. She is the author of *The Romance of Risk: Why Teenagers Do the Things They Do* and *The Sex Lives of Teenagers: Revealing the Secret World of Adolescent Boys and Girls.*

Dr. Ponton works primarily with adolescents, focusing on risk behaviors such as sexual experimentation and eating disorders. She is widely published in scholarly journals and textbooks and has been interviewed for numerous television and radio shows, magazines, and newspapers.

Dr. Ponton is currently working on two projects: her first novel, which follows four generations of adolescents in the Métis culture, and a book on practicing adolescent psychotherapy. The mother of two young adult daughters, Dr. Ponton lives in San Francisco.

Table of Contents

Family Time

Your daughter's most important task right now: to create her own identity, separate from yours and her siblings'.

During her tween years, your daughter is searching for her unique sense of self. During this process she is discovering her own beliefs, values, talents, and desires. Sounds beautiful, doesn't it? But in reality you may hear something like this:

"Leave me alone!"

"Don't try to run my life."

"Stop snooping!"

"I'm not a baby. Don't treat me like one!"

Those cries are the sounds of your daughter wrenching herself away from your protection and control. She is learning to find her own way in the world and to develop confidence that she can survive outside the protective family circle. You can help your daughter through her separation struggles by reassuring her that the inner turmoil she is experiencing is normal and healthy.

Dr. Evelyn Bassoff

TRY THIS

When she pushes you away with angry words, try saying something like, "I'm sorry that you're having a rough time. We probably both need a little space from each other now." With this, you encourage her to get hold of her emotions and sort things out. You also give yourself a welcome time-out.

When both of you have calmed down, you might try saying, "It's like this between mothers and daughters—we're happy to be together sometimes and really angry other times. I know that you're feeling all sorts of pressures and that what I do or say can make you feel worse. But being a mom is hard, too." These words leave her room to apologize or to open up. They also remind her that you have feelings.

Learn to take your daughter's rejections of you less personally. It's the parent part, not the human part, that she's pushing away. This is especially true for girls and their mothers.

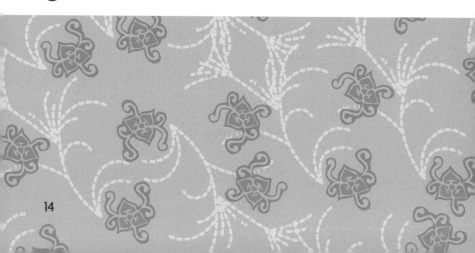

Your daughter's insults, eye rolling, and disapproval will sting less when you remember that she has to find fault with you; if you remained perfect in her eyes, she'd never muster the courage to leave you.

And leaving you, to stand on her own two feet, is ultimately what lies at the end of the tunnel of adolescence.

You can survive this tumultuous time by accepting that this "rubber-band relationship" is the paradox of tween girlhood. One minute your daughter will be friendly and the next she'll become rejecting. This will be less confusing and hurtful if you remind yourself that she wants to be part of the family *and* she wants to be on her own. It will also help to remember that even when she's pushing you away, she still craves your approval.

Dr. Evelyn Bassoff

TRY THIS

"I can see you don't like my (fill in the blank with hair, clothing, jokes, dancing in the kitchen, etc.). You don't have to. You've got your own style, and I've got mine. We're different people. I really like the way (fill in with something about her that you approve of)."

"You don't have to like my style, but please don't say things or give me looks that hurt my feelings. That's just not fair, and you know I try not to insult you."

"Can you say it again without the hurtful part?"

More than anyone else in the world, a mother threatens her daughter's struggle to become an adult.

"Who, me?" moms might ask. "Me, who would protect my daughter with my very life—who, in fact, did that before she was born?"

Yes, exactly. It's not because mothers connive to hold their daughters back. It's because we are continual reminders that not so long ago, they were part of us—safe, warm, and shielded from the outside world.

For young girls, growing up means they have to give up their childish dependence on us, although part of them secretly still wants it. To this end, they create distance between themselves and us.

Dr. Evelyn Bassoff

TRY THIS

Give your daughter space to discover who she is—*literal* space, as in square footage.

Respect her room as her individual space. If you haven't done so already, it's time to knock before you enter, let her close the door, and let her follow her own notions about décor. Give her a budget for things like curtains or new wall color. And no matter what she chooses (and even if you know she'll tire of it), say, "Terrific. It's so you."

Experiment together with color and clothes. There are colors that complement your skin and hair and colors that complement hers. When you're choosing clothing online or in a store, say things like, "That bright color is perfect with your eyes." Or, "That color makes your skin glow. I wish I could wear it, but I need colors that are softer."

Show your daughter you respect her opinions, even if they differ from yours. Seek out her ideas about everything from pop stars to politics, and let her know that you're taking her seriously.

Good news for dads: mothers often bear the brunt of their daughter's developmental anger.

A dad and a daughter may often butt heads, but, because of her gender, a young girl feels inherently different from her male parent. So a girl doesn't have to struggle to disidentify with her father as she does with her mother.

Around Dad a daughter can relax. At times, she may find it easier to accept his guidance, support, and advice than Mom's.

During stormy tween and teenage years, Dad can provide a safe harbor—a place to go when the relationship with Mom is too intense.

Even when a daughter turns to Dad, though, she doesn't want him to make digs against Mom. Girls want—and need—their parents to be one another's biggest fans.

Dr. Evelyn Bassoff

TRY THIS

Dad, your daughter needs you during adolescence more than ever before.

Pick something you and she can share—something for just the two of you. Maybe it's camping, playing a board game, listening to music, making spaghetti, going to ball games, playing computer games, doing yard work, or working on the car. Set that activity aside as dad-daughter time.

It's a pleasure to listen to your daughter when she says something that makes you proud.

It's another story when she attacks your beliefs, complains, or tells you how miserable she is.

When your daughter lashes out at you, rants, or shares a black mood, behind her complaints is an internal conversation. She is asking herself, "Can my mom and dad accept me and love me even if I'm not living my life to please them?" Internally, she may be feeling, "Are Mom and Dad strong enough to be there for me when I'm in trouble, or will I end up taking care of them because they're so upset about me?"

If you really want your daughter to talk about what is going on in her life, learn to stay as calm as possible when she opens up.

Just as you can soothe your daughter, you can soothe yourself by calling on your gentle or lighthearted inner voice. Remind yourself that this too shall pass. When you're anxious, tell yourself, "It's all right. Take a deep breath," and "Whoever said that raising kids would be easy?"

Dr. Evelyn Bassoff

TRY THIS

During tough conversations, say, "Breathe" aloud—both for yourself and for your daughter.

Then listen more than you speak. When you're in doubt or overwhelmed by feelings, ask a question about her feelings or her thoughts. Listen for the emotions as much as for the content.

Remind her that she has some control over tough situations by asking, "What are your choices at this point?"

You can build her resilience by saying, "Today everything went wrong, but you can make a fresh start tomorrow." Remind her that we all make mistakes, and assure her that the emotional pain she's suffering now is not permanent by suggesting, "The one thing we can be sure of is change."

Sometimes it's tempting to not set and enforce limits— we may be afraid that if we do, our daughters will hate us, blow up, or run away.

Research tells us that adolescents grow up to be socially responsible, independent, and self-confident when parents do two things: give loads of affection and set clear limits. Your love for her cannot be shaken. Tell her so. And balance that assurance with limits that keep her emotionally and physically safe.

When your daughter reaches the tween years, around age nine or ten, the words "do it because I say so" are almost certain to backfire. Instead, when she resists a limit you've set, ask questions such as, "How might that work?" or "What can you tell me that would reassure me that changing the rule would be good for you and for our family?"

By negotiating with her, you show her that you take her ideas seriously and that she has the power to influence you if her arguments are persuasive.

However, negotiating doesn't mean you forego clear limits. And while you may choose to explain why you set rules, never apologize for them. For example, say, "That's not a movie you can see. It contains too much violence."

Dr. Evelyn Bassoff

TRY THIS

Listen and validate. Even if you don't agree with her, be willing to see her point of view. You might say, "Yes, I can see that having an earlier curfew than your friends makes you feel babyish." Validating is not the same as giving in.

Require respect. If a discussion turns nasty with yelling or name-calling, stop the talk immediately. Say, "I'm calling a time-out. We'll continue later when we can show each other some respect."

Give yourself time to think. If you're not sure how to respond to a request, say, "I can't give an answer yet. I need to think it over."

If your daughter has lied to you in the past, she'll have to work to regain your confidence by being honest.

It's only when you trust her that she can trust herself.

Your daughter may act as though she couldn't care less about your opinions of her, but the truth is, she cares a great deal. And if you don't trust your daughter, she can't help believing that she'll mess up. That's why the bottom line of so many arguments is, "Why can't you just trust me?"

No matter what rational boundaries you set for your daughter, chances are there will come a time when she defies them. She may go someplace with her friends after you told her not to, or she may lie about who she's been with or how she spent an evening.

Some amount of deception is to be expected during adolescence. Your daughter might lie because she needs privacy or is protecting a friend, or because she wants to try something new and feels you are too restrictive. As a result, she takes a risk as an attempt to get more freedom and move toward independence.

More than anything, you want to trust that the decisions your daughter makes will keep her safe. If you take every opportunity to validate her when she shows good judgment, acts responsibly, thinks things through, handles crises, or copes with hardship, you reinforce her trustworthiness.

Dr. Evelyn Bassoff

TRY THIS

"I do not want to argue with you about whether you lied. But I do want to talk about what it does to our relationship if I feel I can't trust you. Can we talk about that?"

"Here's the bottom line. I can often tell when you're lying." Say no more. Be quiet. Let her come to you when she's ready.

"More than anything in this world I love you and want you to be safe. Please do not lie to me about things you do that might be dangerous."

How you interact with your daughter's father or mother influences your daughter's expectations for herself.

If your daughter sees her parents treat each other with respect, she is more likely to model and expect this behavior in her relationships. She will learn by example that commitments are real, promises are kept, and conflicts are resolvable.

Do all you can to nurture your relationship with your partner by going on regular dates, even though that's hard with work to do and children to raise. If you are no longer with your daughter's other parent, go out of your way to say positive things about him or her. Your daughter comes from both of you, and her self-esteem goes up when both of you are valued.

Dr. Evelyn Bassoff

TRY THIS

Point out things you appreciate about your daughter's other parent. You might say, "I appreciate the way your dad picks you up from school and takes you to practice. Then I can work late when I need to." Or, "I am grateful that your mom is always willing to talk about things." This helps your daughter recognize and appreciate considerate behavior in the relationships she forms.

When you do voice criticism, keep it specific rather than global. For example, saying, "Your dad forgot to put that appointment on the calendar" gives your daughter an entirely different message than saying, "He doesn't care, so he always forgets."

If you are divorced or divorcing, don't let your daughter get caught in a crossfire of hostilities.

During her tween years, a girl is asking who she is. She needs a fan club to encourage her to reach her full potential. If her two main fans—her parents—are busy fighting with each other or emotionally unavailable to her, her fan club disappears. A girl in this situation may grow sad or defiant or may start taking care of everybody else.

This is when you must remember that you and your former (or soon-to-be former) spouse are her main supports. Provide as much stability as you can for your daughter, and don't pressure her to reject the other parent. She needs you both right now.

Although you may secretly hope the other parent falls off the face of the earth, your daughter's self-image and emotional health will always be tied to her relationship with both of you. She needs to be loved by both of you and to love you both.

Dr. Evelyn Bassoff

TRY THIS

Shield your daughter from your own emotional upsets. Take your problems to your friends, your religious community, or your therapist instead.

Assure your daughter that even if there are hard feelings between you and her other parent now, everyone is working toward forgiveness. Try saying something like, "A divorce hurts everyone. We're all in pain right now, but one day not so long from now, it will be better."

The failure of your marriage does not doom your daughter to failed relationships.

Although some children of divorce become cynical about love and marriage, many others do not lose their capacity for enduring, intimate relationships. In fact, living through a divorce and the human pain that accompanies it may result in greater compassion and psychological understanding in some children of divorce.

Of course, your daughter will feel the loss of family as she knew it. Be mindful of this, and seek ways to assure her of your love.

Dr. Evelyn Bassoff

TRY THIS

During a divorce, daughters need their parents' support more than ever. American Girl's book *A Smart Girl's Guide to Her Parents' Divorce* closes by offering girls a "bill of rights." Review it here and do your best to offer your daughter what she is due.

1. I have a right to feel the way I feel about my parents' divorce.

2. I have a right to say what I think and speak up when things are bothering me.

3. I have a right to ask questions and get answers about our family's future.

4. I have a right not to feel guilty about the divorce.

5. I have a right to have a continuing relationship with both of my parents.

6. I have a right not to take sides. I'm free to be loyal and loving to both my parents.

7. I have a right not to hear my parents say bad things about each other.

8. I have a right to say no to a parent who tries to use me as a messenger or a spy or who gets me involved in disagreements about money.

9. I have a right to feel safe.

10. I have a right to celebrate big days and holidays without worrying.

11. I have a right to find help if I need it.

12. I have a right to be proud of my family and to look forward to a happy future.

Credit: From *A Smart Girl's Guide to Her Parents' Divorce*, by Nancy Holyoke. ©/TM 2009 by American Girl, LLC.

It is torture to watch your daughter struggle with grief.

But even if you could shelter her completely, that wouldn't be a good idea.

As painful as it is to see your daughter grieve for a family member who has died, this is a time when, with your guidance, she will learn vital lessons about death, mourning, and giving and receiving comfort.

When someone she knows dies, your daughter may feel angry at the world, at God, at herself, even at the person (or beloved pet) who died and abandoned her.

Because other people can be intolerant of anger in girls, do your best to accept and understand her fury. Assure her that crying is not babyish and can be a great relief.

Dr. Roni Cohen-Sandler

TRY THIS

Hugs. Give your grieving daughter a hug every single day. She may resist, but in reality she needs connection with you.

Ceremony. If your daughter will be attending a funeral or a wake, let her know what to expect. Teach her the power of simply holding the hand of a bereaved person and saying, "I'm sorry for your loss."

Action. When she helps you send a condolence card, shop for groceries for the deceased's family, or make a scrapbook about the person she lost, she learns to cope actively with her own grief.

Her Changing Body & Mind

If your daughter feels awkward about her changing body, she can become fearful about what it's like to grow up.

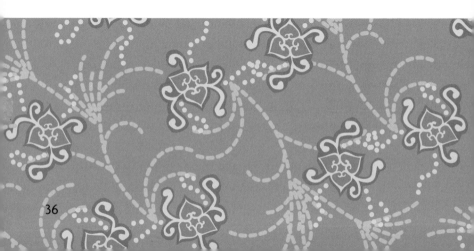

Conflicting messages from friends, magazines, movies, and television can add to your daughter's confusion about what is expected of her in adolescence. Your best gift to her is your willingness to discuss what is going on inside her body, her brain, and her heart.

She will not turn to you with every question that's on her mind, and that's O.K. But you want her to know that *you* know what's going on in the world, that you have accurate information about development and sexuality, and that you love to talk to her when she has questions or concerns.

Don't expect her to bring up her emotions or personal issues, however, if *you* do not model talking about feelings. Show a willingness to discuss all sorts of topics, both physical and emotional.

Dr. Lynda Madison

TRY THIS

Clothing that fits well and flatters is especially important to a girl when her body is changing. Go out of your way to identify shops or online sites that carry clothing neither too babyish nor too mature for her. If she chooses very tight clothing, try not to embarrass her about what it reveals. Instead, focus on whether or not she can move, run, and be herself in those garments.

Continue to snuggle with her and hug her whenever she wants. Warm, respectful touching sends a strong message that her body is O.K., even when she feels confused by how it is changing.

Try not to say, "You're too old for that." A 12-year-old may find solace in something simple like coloring when no one is around to remind her of her age. She may want to climb trees, jump into a pile of leaves, or ride down the hill in her old wagon. Cheer her on.

Invite her to come to you with questions by saying, "I might not know the answer, but we can look it up."

Avoid making comments about your daughter's body.

Affectionate nicknames such as "Skinny Minnie" or "String-bean" may seem harmless now but could set your daughter up for hurt later. When her body starts to fill out, your daughter may then question, "Am I still going to get attention for how I look?" and she may feel pressured to retain her childlike thinness.

Similarly, "Chunky Monkey" or "Pudge" may not get a reaction from her now, but those nicknames may echo in her mind for years to come.

Nicknames can take on a hurtful connotation you didn't intend, and she may end up feeling betrayed by you. Make an effort to praise your daughter (and other people in the family) for things she can do, not for how she looks.

Patti Kelley Criswell, MSW

TRY THIS

Make it clear that appearance is not the top priority in your family.

Make a game of asking family members to describe themselves with five words that have nothing to do with their appearance.

Compliment your daughter's infectious laugh, her ability to make friends, her sports prowess, or her math smarts—everything except her changing body shape.

Your daughter can begin to develop a negative body image at a young age. Once those ideas take root, like weeds, they're very hard to get rid of.

When girls are between seven and nine years old, they become more aware of their own bodies and the bodies of others. They form conclusions about how their bodies look and how they "should" look.

This is the time to tune in to how your daughter talks about her own body, how it looks to her, and how she thinks it compares to others'.

Teach her that there will always be people with bigger bodies and people with smaller bodies, but what matters most is that she likes who she is. Which of her physical features does she like best? Help her to see that it's our differences that make us interesting. Accepting herself and being proud of what makes her unique will help her weather the storms ahead.

Patti Kelley Criswell, MSW

TRY THIS

If she says, "I'm fat" or "I'm skinny," say, "Here's what matters: are you strong?" If she has trouble finding clothes that fit, feel free to discuss designers when you shop together. Try, "Who on earth thought this up?" and you may have more laughs than tears in the dressing room.

If she makes disparaging comments about her body, remind her that it is changing fast and won't be the same in a couple of months.

Build activity into your family life. Help her focus on what her body can do. That means helping her climb hills and trees and ride her bike. When she runs (or climbs or skis or plays soccer), it's as though each stride (or step or swoosh or kick) says "I can." That builds a positive message in her brain. What her body does changes her thinking about how her body looks.

Mom, your daughter will watch you closely for clues about how she should act and feel about being a woman.

Watch what you say about yourself.

Comments such as "I'm so fat" and critical messages on the fridge meant to curb your own eating can harm your daughter. If you diet, do so discreetly.

Take time to examine your own attitudes about weight. If you have a love-hate relationship with your body, work hard not to pass on those feelings to your daughter.

Patti Kelley Criswell, MSW

TRY THIS

Each time you look in the mirror, find something you like about your appearance. Do this for your daughter's sake. It works like osmosis. The better you feel about your body, the better she will feel about hers.

Talk about sizing when you shop together. Explain to your daughter that there are no uniform measurements for clothing sizes; a size 10 from one clothing brand can fit the same as a size 8 from another. Talk about how, very often, the more expensive the store, the smaller the size you seem to be.

Teach your daughter to love good food! Avoid making "healthy" food sound like a bad thing. When you cook "heart smart" lighter recipes, use flavorful spices, and talk to your daughter about the seasonings as you're cooking or eating. Reinforce that you can be healthy and strong and still enjoy food.

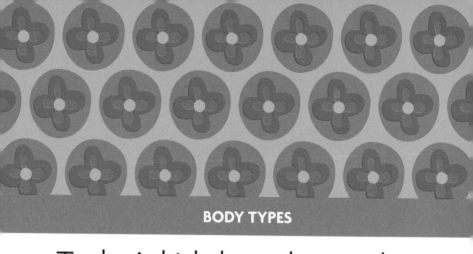

Today's kids have learned not to make fun of someone's ethnicity.

Now, with obesity at record highs, they need to learn not to make fun of body size.

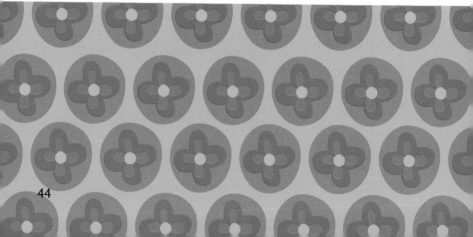

Talk with your daughter about diversity in body types and about not "judging a book by its cover."

As a rule, avoid making comments about other people's bodies in the presence of your daughter. If she makes comments about other people's figures, explain that body shape comes from our ancestry and the culture within our homes.

Remind your daughter that when we make fun of someone else's body, not only is it cruel, but it's also a bullying behavior and absolutely unacceptable. Teach her how to change the subject and not join in when others start hurtful teasing. Be sure to express your own compassion for people who have obvious health problems, including weight problems.

Patti Kelley Criswell, MSW

TRY THIS

The next time you're in the mall, an airport, or another busy place together, have your daughter look around at all of the different body types you see there. Be sure she notes that very few people look like rail-thin models.

Some evening when you're outside with your daughter, as the sun moves toward setting, look at how your shadows stretch long on the ground. Play "shadow tag" together. Afterward, move your body in different positions and point out the way your shadow changes from elongated to squat. Guide your daughter to the idea that the shapes of our bodies are not who we are.

Always point out women who have personal style and individuality. Say, "She doesn't try to look like anyone else. She has her own style. So do you."

If your daughter thinks her looks are the key to her popularity, she may feel she has to behave or dress provocatively to maintain her self-worth.

Sexy styles and images are everywhere—in movies and music, in clothing stores for young women, and even on toy shelves.

If your daughter decides she needs to conform to provocative styles at a young age, not only will she receive attention from boys for which she is not prepared, but she may also leave her peers behind and miss out on the support she would receive from other girls.

Help your daughter understand that dressing provocatively sends a message that she wants others to judge her on her sexiness rather than on her personality and accomplishments. Prove that you value her, too, and not just for how she looks but also for who she is and how she thinks, acts, and treats other people.

Dr. Lynda Madison

TRY THIS

Watch movies with your daughter. Talk to the screen. If the princess is weak or waiting to be rescued, suggest that she do something to help herself out of the jam she's in. Cheer on female characters who have spunk.

Seek out books and movies about strong men and women. Share those stories with your daughter. Introduce her to your friends who do interesting things with their lives. Give her lots of opportunities to talk with those friends.

If your daughter wears outfits that seem provocative, ask her, rather than tell her, what messages she thinks those styles send. Try something like, "What message do you think someone might get when they see you wearing that at school?"

Then listen closely. Gently let her know that the message she means to send might not be the message others will read or receive. When necessary, prohibit her wearing provocative clothing with, "It's not up for further discussion right now. It's my job as your parent to protect you."

If you don't point out the inappropriateness of demeaning messages about women, she is likely to believe that you approve—and agree.

This is true for both mothers and fathers.

Dads, you can help steer your daughter's focus to things other than physical appearance and boys, such as how enjoyable she is to be around and how skilled she is at sports or math. When you pay attention to her for her personality and skills, she learns that you value who she is, the activities she tries, and the things she accomplishes. As a man, you can also give her perspective about the attitudes some boys may have toward girls, and guide her about how to respond to those attitudes.

Dr. Lynda Madison
Patti Kelley Criswell, MSW

TRY THIS

Teach your daughter to be an informed consumer. Mute TV commercials and talk with your daughter when ads feature emaciated body types or women in harmful relationships.

Point out how advertisers target girls' insecurities to get them to buy products. Laugh with your daughter at the absurdity of the promises ads make. Try something like, "Oh yes, that makeup will totally change my life!"

These conversations are generally relaxed and easy to have when she's seven or eight years old, but in a few years, the pull from her peers may compete with your words. You can lay the groundwork today for the pressures that will hit later. Don't get discouraged. She will always hear your voice in her head commenting on images that are harmful or untrue.

Watch for inappropriate books, magazines, movies, and music in your home. And don't just take some rating service's word for what's appropriate. Know what she is listening to and looking at, and give her input about the messages these media send.

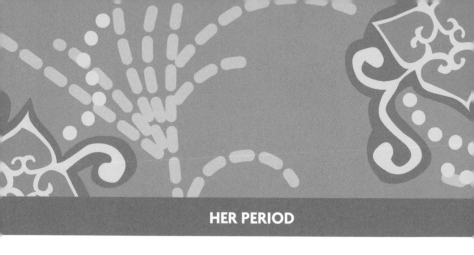

Your daughter may view puberty as a competition. Who is developing first? Who has started her period?

Girls obviously develop at different rates, but they all go through the same general stages. Here's a refresher.

Somewhere between the ages of eight and thirteen, a girl's brain releases a chemical called gonadotropin-releasing hormone, or GNRH, which signals her body to begin to mature. Her hands, legs, and feet grow first, which can cause some awkwardness as she gets used to these changes.

Most girls get a growth spurt during puberty. They grow rapidly for two to three years. About the time the growth spurt begins, a girl's breasts and pubic hair will begin to develop.

You can help your daughter adjust by reassuring her that the changes her body is, or will be, experiencing are normal—no matter what their pace.

Dr. Lynda Madison

TRY THIS

When your daughter is around eight years old, speak to her casually about the fact that girls get their periods and that they get them at different ages. Let her know that her period is likely to still be a ways off but that you'll help her be ready when it starts.

As the time gets closer, buy the supplies she'll need so that they'll be on hand when she needs them. Help her make a plan for what to do if she gets her period at school (have supplies in her locker, get supplies from the nurse, tie a sweater around her waist to cover any spotting).

Remind her that she can ask you anything and that you'll give her an honest answer. When she does ask questions, do not feel that you need to tell her everything. Just answer the question she asks and then ask, "Anything else?"

The Stages of Puberty: A Refresher

Your daughter may be reading books about puberty, such as American Girl's *The Care & Keeping of You*, which breaks down adolescent growth into five stages. Knowing these stages can help you better relate to your daughter's thoughts and concerns.

Stage One: Before Puberty. The breast area and nipples are level with the chest. The circle around the nipple, the *areola*, is small and light. No pubic hair is present.

Stage Two: Early Puberty. The breast and nipple rise in a small mound that some call a *breast bud*. The circle of the areola gets larger and often darker. Soft, fine hair grows in the center of the pubic area.

Stage Three: Middle Puberty. This stage usually begins a few months to a year after Stage Two starts. The breast and areola get larger, the areola gets darker, and breasts become pointier. More pubic hair grows.

Stage Four: Late Puberty. The areola and nipple rise above the level of the breast to form a separate curve. Pubic hair now covers more of the pubic area but less than an adult's hair will.

Stage Five: Adulthood. The breast is mature, having a fuller and rounder appearance. The nipple sticks out. The areola is level with the rest of the breast. Pubic hair forms the shape of an upside-down triangle and spreads to the thighs.

Credit: From *The Care & Keeping of You*, by Valorie Lee Schaefer. ©/TM 1998 by American Girl, LLC.

Girls may become concerned if they lag behind their friends, especially because development is so often part of their conversation.

If your daughter is slow to develop, she may feel embarrassed and insecure.

She will need your reassurance that she is likely to catch up to her peers and that there are other important areas—such as academics, sports, or hobbies—on which to focus her attention while she waits.

Dr. Lynda Madison

TRY THIS

Buy her a bra, even if she's flat chested. If she is really self-conscious about being behind the other girls, a bra with a little bit of padding might help her feel more comfortable.

If she is very concerned, however, talk with her doctor before she goes for a checkup. Ask the doctor to reassure her that she is normal and that she will develop with time.

Mention the good things that go along with having smaller breasts, such as freedom of movement during sports.

If late development runs in your family, express your empathy. Try, "I remember how it was. It seemed as if I'd never grow. Then suddenly I did, and so will you."

Remind her dad to compliment her on all the appropriate things—her energy, her eyes, her laugh, her brains, her character, and her agility.

Girls who develop early often face pressures other girls don't experience until they are older.

It's not easy being an early bloomer.

Girls who look older than their peers can get treated as if they are older and face more teasing and unwanted attention than their friends.

This kind of teasing can cause some girls to be fearful in school and lack confidence in themselves. You can help your daughter cope with any unkind comments from others or stressful situations that might arise.

Dr. Lynda Madison

TRY THIS

Talk with your daughter about how to handle unwelcome sexual attention and how to stay safe. Give her words to say if she is harassed, such as, "Stop it!" "I don't like that," and "I said 'No.' " Suggest several adults at her school to whom she can turn if she ever feels uneasy.

If your daughter has older brothers, be sure they never tease her about her body. Tell them it is their job to model respectful behavior toward her.

If you're a dad, be sure to tell her that she is precious to you. And say, "If someone makes rude comments to you or makes you feel uncomfortable, come and tell me. That's never O.K." Never hesitate to intercede. She should not have to deal with unwanted sexual attention alone.

Be your daughter's ally around others. If friends or relatives haven't seen her for a while and assume she is older than her age, their attention may make her uncomfortable. Gently remind them that she is not even a teenager yet. A simple statement like, "She's only ten" can help keep their comments age appropriate.

Tween girls crave predictability and security; that's one reason your daughter may react to difficult situations as if her very world is caving in around her.

As girls adjust to dramatic changes in their bodies, emotional lives, schools, and friendships, coping with distressing life events—real or imagined—can be especially hard.

Learning to master stressful experiences will definitely help your daughter grow and mature, but when she faces tough situations for the first time, she may become anxious, self-doubting, over-wrought, or helpless when she most wants to feel in control. Feelings are contagious within families, so her upset can be up-setting for both of you.

When strong feelings make your daughter feel as though she is spinning out of control, do your best to respond calmly. It is reassuring for her to learn from you that her reactions, even if they are painful, are normal. Empathizing with her—long before any problem solving begins—is key.

Dr. Roni Cohen-Sandler

TRY THIS

Listen to her story. Then help her name the specific emotions she is experiencing. Is she angry, afraid, anxious, or jealous? Lonely, grieving, or mad? Simply naming her feelings gives her some sense of control.

Use your physical presence to help her find center again. If you sit still and breathe deeply as you look directly into her eyes and listen to her story, she will unconsciously begin to breathe with you and soak in your calm. You may want to ask, "May I hug you?" or "Want me to rub your back?" if those are things that help her calm down.

Validate her feelings. Try, "I can see why you feel upset/angry/sad." Do not try to talk her out of her feelings, but help her move past them when she's ready by asking, "What could we do that would help you feel better?" Suggest an activity like baking together, taking a walk, calling her granddad, or giving the dog a bath.

The more you listen to her,
the more she hears you.

Communication between you and your daughter may close down at the very time you want to prepare her for the world outside her home. But what she needs right now, more than your advice, is your sympathetic ear. How can you be a really good listener?

1. Accept that good listening can feel risky when you're used to a "what-I-say-goes" stance.
   • Be interested in her ideas and listen without judgment.
   • Be prepared to let her change your mind.

2. Give her your undivided attention.
   • Turn off the TV, cell phone, and computer.
   • Make eye contact. It tells her, "Yes, I'm here. I'm paying attention to you."

3. Make your goal to understand, not to score points. Refrain from:
   • interrupting, contradicting, and debating;
   • launching into a discussion about yourself when your daughter is talking.

Dr. Evelyn Bassoff

TRY THIS

Good listening doesn't mean you have to sit in silence with an approving grin as she chatters on. Always ask questions; then she knows you're listening.

You can say, "I'm not sure I understand. Could you give me another example or say it in another way?" Make sure you're on track: "It sounds to me as if you're saying (fill in the blank). Am I right? If I'm misunderstanding you, tell me what I'm getting wrong."

When she tells you something that's obviously a new thought for her, give her credit for her growing intellect. Try, "This is interesting. You are able to compare things (or analyze or solve problems) in ways you couldn't when you were younger."

Withdrawal and rudeness are not always signs that your daughter is shutting you out—but they sure can make it feel that way.

Hormones can contribute to your daughter's moodiness during her tween years, but anxiety and uncertainty play big roles, too. It's natural to feel dismayed by your daughter's angry words, demands to be left alone, or melodramatic expressiveness.

Stay as calm as you can during the storm. Most likely your daughter is vacillating between wanting to be older and wishing she could stay secure as your little girl. Don't let your anger, disappointment, or resentment of her moodiness weaken the communication you have with her.

Setting boundaries and consequences for her is important, but so is gentle reassurance that her experiences are normal and that you are not going to abandon her just because she is going through a moody spell.

Dr. Lynda Madison

TRY THIS

First, ask her to describe the situation and what she thinks might happen next. Knowing where she is coming from can help you know how to help.

Rather than assuming her emotions, ask what she is feeling. She could be feeling many different things and not be able to describe the subtle differences between disappointment and embarrassment, anger and hurt. You can help her find the right words.

Sit with her along with her emotions, but don't belabor the situation. Let her know that you've had disappointments, too, and life doesn't always seem fair, but there is something to be learned from every situation. Let her know that you hope she will try again, perhaps another way, another time.

When it's appropriate, keep things light. As a family, it can be fun to come up with language that helps you talk about moods. Then you can talk in family code such as, "Feeling pink today?" or "Boy, I'm so orange." This might help everyone talk about their moods in an enjoyable, nonaccusatory way.

Friends,
Bullies & Boys

At some point, you may feel abandoned by your daughter—replaced in your VIP role by her friends. You're not alone.

When your daughter was younger, she told you about her every sadness and joy. But as she gets older, it's likely she prefers spending more time with her friends. The page turns for her, and parents have to accommodate that change. It's part of how girls grow.

So, plan on it: your daughter will take friends into her heart while excluding you. And, in time, she'll bring her heart to you for mending when it gets broken by those same friends. Fortunately, this is evidence that she is developing right on schedule. It means you've done your job well, preparing her to risk, trust, and love.

During these years, you become an on-call parent. You begin wearing an emotional beeper, so to speak. You're always available. When your daughter beeps you—and she will—you drop every-thing, help her pull herself together, and send her out into the world of peers and friendships again.

As the circle of a girl's life gets bigger, an on-call parent under-stands that the circle doesn't exclude him or her. It simply contains more people than before.

Amy Lynch
Patti Kelley Criswell, MSW

TRY THIS

Watch for check-ins. Maybe your daughter will give you an unex-pected hug, ask you for help, or even pick a quick fight with you. These are all check-ins. She's making sure you're still there—the base from which she takes off and to which she always returns, if only to push off again. This part of your job is easy: just be there for her.

During this period of her life, agree on something special the whole family will do together regularly—pizza and games one night a week or an evening that's technology-free (no cell phones or MP3 players). This helps balance friend time with family time.

Riding the fierce emotional waves of friendships is good practice for your daughter in negotiating relationships.

As girls grow older, they become more selective in their friendships, choosing fewer friends to spend time with and getting to know them better. Best friends become more important. In these tight relationships, girls learn about each other in depth. An intense friendship is an early form of an intimate relationship with someone outside a girl's family.

Don't be surprised when your daughter's friendships and loyalties change. Pay attention to your daughter's cues. Expect her friendships to run hot and cold, sometimes alternating quite rapidly, and check out the current status before you comment on anything. Otherwise you may get pushed away for not understanding.

Virginia Beane Rutter, MS

TRY THIS

Want to know a little more about your daughter's shifting friendships? Try asking her to identify her friends to you in "texting" language. For example, her best friend forever is "BFF." The girl she was friends with over the summer might be "LBSF" (Lena, Best Summer Friend). Her friend from gymnastics might be "TWBL" (Toby with the Big Laugh). This system can be fun, helps you learn a little more about her friends, and helps you sort things out if several of her friends have the same name.

The more often you talk with your daughter about her friendships, the more free she may feel to come to you with friendship problems or questions. When she does, listen patiently. Help her write down different solutions to her problem or actions she could take. Next (even if it feels goofy) help her act out some of the scenarios and actually say the words she wants to try out. A few practice rounds will have her ready to try it on her own.

Mom, you will always be a role model for your daughter's relationships with her friends.

Even as your daughter's friends begin to play more important roles in her life, you are still her primary role model. Who are your good friends? What are your relationships with them like?

Your daughter wants to see that friends have a place in your life. She, too, will build support systems that will hold her through difficult times. As these relationships gel, she will go back and forth between you and them. Ultimately, her relationship with you enhances her other relationships—and vice versa.

Virginia Beane Rutter, MS

TRY THIS

We all go through major changes as our daughters are growing up, including changes in our own friendships.

Consider how you speak about your friends. Are you giving your daughter positive messages? Each time you say, "I'm so lucky to have good friends I can talk to," she feels more certain of finding good friends, too.

On the other hand, if you put down and criticize your own friends, this teaches your daughter to expect and do the same. Our daughters imitate us, even when we (and they) don't know it.

Walk a fine line between allowing your daughter to choose her own friends and being aware of who they are and what they are up to.

After a long day at work, extra kids in your house may feel like an invasion of your space. But making your home a welcoming place for your daughter's friends means that you get to know them. Talk to them, and they'll talk to you.

Don't hesitate to talk with other parents and with teachers about the kids your daughter spends time with. If your daughter objects to this, just say, "Honey, it's what parents do," and let it go. As parents today, we're much more involved in our daughters' lives than our own parents tended to be. Times have changed, and knowing her friends, and about her friends, is an essential part of being an engaged parent.

If you're talking with your daughter and her friends and something startles you in someone's behavior, dress, or language, be observant and neutral. Ask questions and listen carefully. If you are reactive, your daughter and her friends may feel compelled to keep things from you that you need to know.

Virginia Beane Rutter, MS

TRY THIS

Say something like, "I enjoyed talking with your friend _____. She/he has . . . (choose one)

a. a good sense of humor."

b. a really kind heart."

c. good stories to tell."

In other words, tell your daughter that you enjoy your talks with her friends, and be specific in your praise. Then say no more. Your daughter will tell you about her friends' faults and poor choices. If you point out those things, your daughter will almost certainly hear your comments as criticism of herself (because she naturally identifies deeply with her friends). Let her criticize her friends while you stand neutral.

Text messages can keep your daughter close to you and to friends. But texting can also do damage in the time it takes to hit "send."

When it comes to knowing your daughter's friends, the "text" feature on the cell phone adds a new and sometimes confusing dimension. When girls are not with their friends, they often check in by sending constant text messages to each other.

When your daughter's friends are at your house, they may be texting at the same time they are talking with you. Things happen quickly in these text messages; news and rumors fly at "thumb speed." Sometimes these messages can feel like secretive whispers to which others in the group are not privy.

Don't hesitate to ask questions about incoming text messages that seem inappropriate or unduly exciting to the group. Explain that if people are reading and sending text messages while they are hanging out with *you*, those messages become part of the group's conversation. In a casual way, ask them to share what is being texted and what the responses are. ("What's going on there, Emily?") Otherwise, like phone calls, secretive text messages can be intrusive, hurtful, or rude.

Amy Lynch

TRY THIS

Rules about sending text are like rules about telephone use. Each family needs its own regulations. Family time and mealtime are probably going to be "no text" zones.

If your daughter has a cell phone, you may want to learn to text if you haven't already done so. That way you and she can exchange information quickly and discreetly when you are not in a situation that lends itself to a phone call. For example, between meetings at work, you might send, "How was practice? R U @ home?" And her "Yes, Patty is cool" reply lets you know that the sitter picked her up and all is well.

Without friends, a girl can fall into a dark abyss; she can feel invisible.

Sometimes a girl just "disappears" in her social milieu—no one texts her in the evening or calls out her name on the school grounds. Or maybe she moves to a new school and nobody reaches out to her right away. During friendless periods, your daughter really needs you. You can be a powerful source of companionship when she's between friends.

Size up the situation as objectively as you can. If your daughter talks about a tragic social faux pas, yet is still surrounded by friends, assure her that her feelings of isolation will pass. If she is hurting, approach her with compassion. Social rejection is often a source of pain and anxiety for girls. It can undermine their confidence in their ability to master new situations.

The easy advice—walk away and look for friendship elsewhere—is not easy to follow. Your daughter may be so crushed that she withdraws instead of reaching out to new friends. Help her as she takes time to recover. Meanwhile, encourage her to find activities in which she will naturally meet new friends.

Virginia Beane Rutter, MS

TRY THIS

Sit with her at night before she goes to sleep. This is when her worst fears and highest hopes tend to emerge. Provide her with soothing, loving ideas at this point in the day. Read good books together. Ask her what she fantasizes about doing as a young adult. Reassure her that she's between friends, not without them. Assure her that a new friend is out there waiting to meet her. It's just a matter of time.

During times of social stress, give her lots to do: new books to read, good movies to watch, special things to do with you, or that new craft kit she's been wanting.

Enlist others in your efforts to keep her busy. Ask her grandfather to take her to hit golf balls. Maybe she and her favorite aunt can see a cool museum exhibit. As adults, we can't replace peers in our daughters' lives, but we can help them through lonely times.

Don't make the mistake of expecting your daughter's friendship groups to be structured like yours were.

Popularity as we knew it when we were kids hardly exists anymore. Our daughters are likely to experience something different—less a social pyramid with the most popular kids on top, more a network of groups of friends with similar interests.

If your 12-year-old doesn't have the giggling, all-girl gang you remember from childhood, not to worry. She may be finding good friends in multiple "friendship pods" instead. Perhaps she knows lots of people—boys and girls alike—and connects deeply with a couple of friends from her sports team, one who shares her interest in Japanese comics, one in her class at school, and two more from summer camp.

Cell phones and computers allow her to stay in touch with all of her friends, even those who live far away. Together, these friends from various groups can form a strong friendship group for your daughter, even though the friends don't know each other. That's 21st-century friendship for you!

Amy Lynch

TRY THIS

Every girl needs face-to-face friends, but provide ways for your daughter to stay in touch with faraway friends who have moved or whom your daughter has met at events, competitions, or camps.

As always, limit cell phone and online time to reasonable hours, but remember that high-tech communication can have a steadying effect on a girl if a supportive friend is typing out the e-mail or sending the text.

Never hesitate to get in touch with the parents of your daughter's friends, no matter where they live, with questions, concerns, or ideas about how the families can connect. Always ask your daughter for the e-mail addresses and phone numbers of her friends' parents. This makes staying in touch easier, and you can be sure you know what's going on, just as you can with parents who live in your community.

Cliques can hurt.

If a girl thinks her only option is to tough it out, she can get in over her head before she knows it.

Studies have shown that all-girl groups tend to work collaboratively more so than groups of boys do. Girls cooperate in class and in team sports, and they are enlivened by working together.

But competition between girls often develops, too—and can get in the way of girls finding friends in whom they can really trust. During adolescence, when girls are exploring their own strengths and weaknesses, they develop a keen radar for other girls' weaknesses. A girl who puts *other* girls down will soon find other girls putting *her* down, and alliances can change rapidly. There's no substitute for a girl having at least one close, true friend by the time she reaches middle school.

If your daughter is unhappy with her social group, help her get out of her normal environment by joining a new activity. If she is continually ostracized or cruelly teased, seek counseling for her.

Virginia Beane Rutter, MS

TRY THIS

Remember that you and your daughter don't have to deal with mean cliques alone. Ask teachers and guidance counselors to raise the standard for kindness within the classroom.

Be her best ally. Assure her daily that she is completely lovable, right down to her toenails.

Let her be angry if that's how she feels. The American Girl book *Stand Up for Yourself & Your Friends* contains a parents' guide that reminds us *not* to rescue our daughter from feeling negative emotions. When she comes to you to let off steam, honor her feelings—whatever they are—instead of talking her out of them.

Try a visualization. Ask her to imagine standing like a tree rooted deep in the earth. Have her name the roots. Maybe she'll say her family, her faith, or people she loves. Suggest that she stand like a tree and think about those roots when she encounters cruel behavior from cliques.

What do parents fear most for their tween daughters?

The answer is often "all the 'mean girl' stuff."

It's true that bullying among young girls is prevalent. The good news: research shows that when children do speak up, bullying stops much more frequently than when they stay quiet.

You can help by raising your daughter to be a good *bystander*, a person who stands up for others who are being mistreated.

Patti Kelley Criswell, MSW

TRY THIS

Help your daughter practice being a good bystander by speaking out against bullying and standing up for other children who are getting bullied. Teach her to distinguish tattling from telling. *Tattling* is done solely to injure someone else's ego or image. *Telling*, or reporting, is done to protect someone who is being hurt by another.

Talk about power. Tell her that when people bully, they are trying to take away someone else's power. If she is bullied, teach her to react in a strong, confident way—to keep her head held high and look annoyed or bored rather than scared or hurt. Help her practice this reaction with you at home. Then she'll be ready when the bullying happens again.

Give her words to say to herself to help her hold the mean behavior at bay. Try, "I won't let other people's bad attitudes rub off on me," or "I can get through this."

If your daughter stands up to a bully, will the bully start to harass her?

Social scientists tell us that bullies are drawn to those whose power they can take away, which makes good *bystanders*—those who speak out against bullying—somewhat "bully-proof."

Also, there's power in numbers. Good bystanders tend to be, and have, loyal friends. The odds of a bully turning on a bystander are significantly lower when the bystander has peer support, so it's worth it for your daughter to spread the word about the need to speak up.

Patti Kelley Criswell, MSW

TRY THIS

American Girl's book *Stand Up for Yourself & Your Friends* includes a guide for parents on helping their daughters handle bullies.

Do not urge her to be "nice" if people are hurting her. Urge her to be strong instead. Ask, "What can you say to them that would be strong without being hurtful?" You might suggest, "I know what you're doing. It won't work. Stop it." Or simply, "Stop, Sarah," using the bully's name.

Teach your daughter to say words such as, "What are you doing?" or "How would you like it if someone said that to you?" Speaking out is an emotional risk, but if she can stand up to a bully in second grade, she'll be able to in seventh, when the stakes are even higher.

Intervene by talking with her teacher. Keep any conversations with the teacher or other parents "facts only"; it's easy for conversations about bullying to become mean-spirited. Have a contact person at school help facilitate interventions.

Teach her how to find allies. She can tell those allies that she is going to speak up the next time something happens. She can tell them that they don't have to say anything if they are afraid, but that she does need them to stand beside her.

When children hear parents gossip or say negative things about others, they come to believe that it's O.K.

Girls in adolescence learn a lot from watching the behavior of others and comparing it to their own. It's natural for your daughter to talk about what other kids do or say, but gossip, with its edge of cruelty, is something different.

During this stage of your daughter's life, you can help her distinguish between the two. Make sure you're setting an example of kindness toward others. Model kind behavior, and be a good bystander yourself.

Patti Kelley Criswell, MSW

TRY THIS

In conversations with your daughter, point out the difference between flat-out gossiping and talking about events, school, or things that are troubling her.

Teach your daughter the difference between venting and gossip. *Venting* is talking with someone who isn't involved in the situation, and it's meant to bring about a resolution. *Gossip* is meant to hurt someone's image, stir up trouble, or spread around negative energy.

If you hear your daughter's observations about someone else stray into gossip, ask, "This sounds really stressful and negative. What can you do to feel better about the situation?"

BOY FRIENDS, NOT BOYFRIENDS

Boys make good friends, too.

These days, it's not uncommon for girls and boys to develop deep nonsexual friendships. Any "posse" of friends today is likely to contain both girls and boys; they talk to each other about everything from algebra homework to family problems.

Having a boy as a friend means your daughter sees boys as regular people, not as creatures from another planet. Just like having brothers, having boys as true friends means that a girl will have fewer misconceptions about boys when she begins having romantic relationships with them.

Virginia Beane Rutter, MS

TRY THIS

Talk, listen, and talk some more with your daughter's friends who are boys. Show an interest in what they're doing and what they're thinking, just as you do with your daughter's friends who are girls. Hang around with open ears.

If your daughter is teased about her "boy friend," remind her that teasers want her to be embarrassed. Her goal should be to *not* cooperate, by staying calm and cool. If people ask her, "Is he your boyfriend?" suggest she look them in the eye and say, "No, we're just friends"—and keep saying that as many times as it takes for them to get bored with the conversation.

No two girls discover romance at the same pace. How will you know what to expect from your daughter?

In their tween years, some girls are just beginning to feel romantic attractions. They have crushes and seem to talk endlessly with friends about the daily activities of boys they know or want to know. Other girls may be uninterested in boys, while still others progress more quickly, having sexual relationships for which they may not be ready.

It's not just our daughters who must be prepared to deal with the emotional and physical issues involving boys, sexual attraction, and romance. We parents have to be ready to support our daughters so that they learn to develop healthy, balanced relationships.

Foster openness with your daughter. Start saying the magic words, "You can ask me anything," when your daughter is young. Keep that message coming as she grows up—even when questions get tougher.

Dr. Lynn Ponton

TRY THIS

If your daughter shows no interest in romantic relationships during her tween years, don't rush her. Trust her to find meaningful relationships when she is ready. In the meantime, if she has a crush on someone, refrain from teasing her. At her age, a crush can be a very real emotional risk. Try not to make comments about the person one way or the other.

If she is feeling down because of something that happened (or didn't happen) with a boy, gently remind her that, although it doesn't seem that way, he really is only one of many people who will spark her interest. If you're her father, assure her that she's a terrific kid and that you're proud to be her dad. You might shed a little light on boys with words like, "At this age, boys don't always recognize a really great girl."

When it comes to talking about sex, the most important "fact of life" is that one talk isn't enough. You'll need many conversations in which you both talk and listen.

When your daughter was younger, answering questions such as "Where do babies come from?" may have seemed tricky but manageable. As she becomes a tween, the conversations can become more difficult. The key—no matter how challenging the conversations are for *you*—is to let your daughter know she can keep talking and asking questions, no matter what.

Don't leave the conversations to someone else. Girls will get information from many sources, so be sure that you are her first source. You can do this by listening carefully and reacting matter-of-factly when she broaches the subject.

Another key is language. Be specific. For example, try not to say "sex" if you mean intercourse or "making out" if you mean touching above the waist.

Most importantly, when talking about sexual activity, stress the emotional impact that it has on the people involved. Be sure to emphasize the way sexual activity affects a girl's emotions. The good news is that girls who have close and open relationships with their parents are more likely to postpone becoming sexually active, and postponement is exactly the result you want.

Dr. Lynn Ponton
Amy Lynch

TRY THIS

If she asks a specific question, answer that question. Resist going into a long lecture. Then ask, "Does that answer your question?" and, "Is there anything else that you want to ask me?"

Think of discussions about sexual activity as part of an ongoing conversation, not something you can do once and check off your list. Use examples from the media and other daily experiences as starters for brief but important talks.

These words may be useful: "Sex is complicated. Lots of rumors about it just aren't true. You can ask me if you have questions."

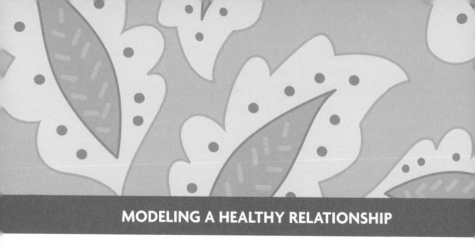

Point out positive aspects of relationships **among the couples you observe in daily life.**

When you highlight the companionship, sharing, and trust you see in couples you know, as well as in your own relationship, you help your daughter understand why relationships are truly valuable, and you teach her what she should look for in her own.

Speak respectfully of your partner, whether or not he or she is in the room. Avoid the urge to let your daughter "in" on jokes or comments about the little things in daily life your partner may do that get under your skin. A decade from now, she'll understand all that, but for right now, she is your daughter, not your girlfriend.

Dr. Lynn Ponton

TRY THIS

When your daughter observes couples and talks with you about them, ask her what she likes about the way they treat each other.

Use happy relationships in your family as teaching examples. You might say, "Granddad and Grandmother are so kind to each other. I've always been touched by that."

If couples in your family or your friendship circle have problems, answer her questions as fairly as possible. State your intolerance for abuse, physical or emotional, within any relationship.

Classroom
Crossroads

School is your daughter's world, where she must step away from your protective arms and make it on her own.

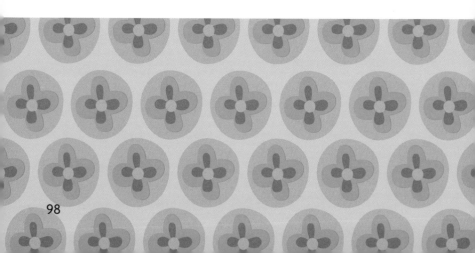

In your daughter's life, school is an incubator for all things exciting, promising, fulfilling, doubt provoking, and sometimes frightening. Your daughter has to speak out, prove herself, and be graded on it to boot. Every day is an exercise, not just in stretching and strengthening her mind, but also in negotiating the social and political circles of her peers.

It can be helpful for your daughter to have an adult—someone she feels cares about her—whom she can talk to about school issues. Help your daughter find "her adult" at school. It can be the nurse, a secretary, or her gym teacher—someone who has a good ear and insight into the workings of her peer group and her class.

Dr. JoAnn Deak

TRY THIS

If your daughter indicates she is trying to sort through the many stimulations, distractions, and expectations in her classroom, she may be looking for guidance. Ask her to make a map of her class for you. Who sits where, and what is each person like? Where does the teacher stand? Where is her favorite activity center? The same goes for the hallways and the cafeteria. Making a map together helps you learn about her environment and, at the same time, gives her a stronger sense of control.

Talk with her teacher. Ask, "How is she in class?" This open-ended kind of question invites the teacher to share the full range of his or her observations with you. If your daughter is struggling to find friends, ask the teacher who might make good friends for your daughter, and suggest to your daughter that she invite over those "potentials."

When your daughter is facing an academic struggle in the classroom, it's hard to know whether to just listen, to offer advice, or to try to fix it.

As tempting as it is to take over and fix your daughter's problems, this is the time to show her all the tools she has in her toolbox. Then she can learn how and what it takes to fix things herself. Start by listening, and keep going gently and carefully, feeling your way until you both are satisfied. The more you fix, the less she learns.

Take a look at your daughter's issue. Does it cause short-term stress that's gone after she achieves the goal (for example, anxiety over an upcoming test)? Afterward, does she feel more confident because of her efforts? Or is her struggle marked by symptoms such as headaches or insomnia?

If the former is the case, you can provide the usual support—helping her use her time wisely, answering questions, or sitting nearby while she studies. But if you see a pattern of anxiety, failure, or both, it's time to do more.

Dr. JoAnn Deak

TRY THIS

Work with your daughter to make a list of resources she can use to help her perform academically. The list might include online sites, you, her teacher, librarians, aids such as timers, and maybe a tutor (perhaps someone a few years older who can help her after school).

If your daughter expresses despair about mastering a certain subject, help her break the subject into small parts. Point out that her textbook is divided into chapters, and she has to learn only one small part at a time. Help her focus on the present. Assure her, "You can get through this day's work. It's all you have to do. I'll help you."

Use standardized tests to your advantage. Girls take annual tests that identify their strengths and weaknesses in specific subject areas and with specific material within those areas. Ask your daughter's teachers to talk with you about what your daughter understands and what she is missing. Then you can work with her in ways that address her problems directly.

Elementary school is like those comfortable old sneakers that are broken in just the way you like them. Middle school is like a new shoe that pinches **all over.**

For girls, the change from elementary school to middle school can be a harsh adjustment. Part of it has to do with the "structure" of elementary and middle schools and the "structure" of girls.

For females, connections with others are the cornerstone of life, and that starts at an early age. Young girls have close relationships with their teachers and classmates. The self-contained classes of the primary grades, with one homeroom teacher and the same classmates all day, feel predictable and safe.

Not so in middle school. As girls move across the fault line between childhood and adolescence, they encounter constant changes and new expectations. Your daughter may also get the classic middle school signals telling her that success lies in not being the smartest kid around.

You can help your daughter across this fault line by staying close, empathizing with her when she worries, and letting her know you have faith in her.

Dr. JoAnn Deak

TRY THIS

Even if she has never been athletic, find something physical she can do now. When a girl is active or competes physically, she feels better about herself.

If she has not yet mastered her school planner or electronic calendar, work with her on this skill. Make sure she knows how to color-code daily tasks and long-term projects.

If you keep a family calendar, add her deadlines to that calendar, too. When the school year begins, sit down with her two or three times a week to go over her planner with her. As her organizational skills grow, you'll do this less often.

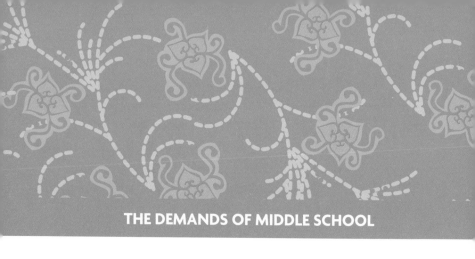

Some girls who used to get everything right in elementary school find middle school more confusing, more demanding, and less fun.

What happened? First, there is the social pressure. Girls often walk a tightrope of appearing smart but not *too* smart so that they will fit in. Some girls continue to get good grades but do it more covertly, participating less visibly in class.

A conceptual shift also happens. The elementary years are designed for "learning to" skills: learning to read, write, and calculate. In middle school, there is a shift to applying what children have learned. They are no longer learning to read; they are reading to learn. They are writing to express thoughts and calculating to problem-solve. This is a huge leap for a young person.

Dr. JoAnn Deak

TRY THIS

Ask. If your daughter's interest in school has waned, talk with her teachers and guidance counselor about what your daughter is like in class. Have they noticed that she is distracted? Have they seen other reasons for her discouragement? Solicit their support.

Celebrate. When your daughter finishes a big project, brings home good grades, or gives a nerve-racking oral report, celebrate her success with a family night, her favorite food, or new tunes for her MP3 player.

Where does the dividing line lie for your daughter between working hard and pushing herself beyond healthy limits?

Many young girls worry about standardized tests and college admission. In this information age, girls have already heard that they need to do well in college or at some other specialized training in order to be successful. And by sixth grade, if not before, most girls feel the pressure to be high achievers.

In fact, many professionals attribute high rates of depression among girls and boys alike to an inability to deal with the ongoing stress of intense learning, testing, sometimes failing, learning more, and testing again.

Amy Lynch

TRY THIS

Provide balance. Some girls have schools and teachers who put them under tremendous pressure to excel, constantly reminding girls that high school, SAT or ACT exams, and college are just around the corner. Other girls are in classrooms where not enough is expected of them. Consider your daughter's personality. Is she driven or relaxed? Challenged or bored? Use your parent time to balance what is happening at school.

If your daughter develops physical symptoms such as headaches on Sunday night or Monday morning, a rash in reaction to anxiety, or symptoms that may be stress related, be gentle with her. Help her find support from her teachers, a therapist, or her pediatrician.

Remember that your model of a balanced life is the best teacher of all. Whenever you incorporate self-care, work you love, and family time into your day, she learns to deal with stress.

Does your daughter dare to climb high, **or is she** afraid to succeed?

Some girls are driven to perform and compete in school and sports, but others are happier with noncompetitive activities. Although we can encourage our daughters to try hard and do a good job, we can't teach them to have a burning competitive drive. It just doesn't work that way.

If your daughter consistently shies away from sports competitions or seems threatened by how she stacks up against kids in the classroom, gently try to find out what is holding her back.

If she makes generalizations such as "I'm just not competitive" or "I don't like sports," she may be covering up feelings of incompetence, performance anxiety, or fear of failure. Build her confidence by starting her off with small hurdles.

Dr. JoAnn Deak

TRY THIS

Explore your daughter's feelings about herself this way: Write her name on a piece of paper, listing each letter in a separate box, as if her name were part of a crossword puzzle. Ask her to expand the puzzle by writing something she is good at, loves to do, or would love to try that starts with a letter in her name. If she does this exercise exuberantly, don't worry about her drive. But if she struggles with identifying things that give her pleasure and a sense of achievement, consider talking with her teacher or a counselor about ways to encourage her.

Be aware of your own attitudes toward competition and success. Do you communicate the thrill of achieving your goals or do you send other, perhaps unconscious, messages?

Contemplate this question: Does your daughter behave as if high achievement will come between you and her, or between her and her friends? Would she benefit from exploring and challenging this feeling?

Less can be more.

Let's check our list: Your daughter is expected to focus on her homework, participate in sports, *and* make her mark in extracurricular activities. How do you keep her from being overscheduled?

Try the salad bar theory. The first few times you visit a salad bar, you tend to take a little of each offering so that you can taste everything. As time goes by, you gradually taste all the items you fancy until, finally, you go straight for what you want.

In elementary school, let her sample interests, and don't apply too much pressure if her passion for certain pursuits waxes and wanes. By middle school, she will need to eliminate some activities to focus on others. But in a world filled with interesting things to do, these choices may not be easy.

Dr. JoAnn Deak

TRY THIS

At the beginning of a season, tell your daughter how many activities she can participate in. Talk about the possibilities and help her choose. Once she has chosen, look at a weekly calendar with her. Mark the days she has free time. Ask, "Is this enough time to relax, read, and recover from all you do?"

If halfway through the season or semester she finds herself overscheduled, try this 1-to-10 game.

• List her activities on a sheet of paper.

• Read the name of each activity aloud and give her 2 or 3 seconds to rate each activity with a number between 1 and 10. (The higher the number, the more she likes that activity.) Tell her to think quickly; the number that comes into her mind is the "right" answer.

• After you work through the list once, do it again. Average each activity's scores together, and encourage her to drop the activity with the lowest average score.

There is a difference between a girl who is thriving and one who is worn out by hurrying from one activity to the next.

In addition to school, girls this age stay busy trying new activities, from dance to arts, team sports, and clubs. And each activity is inevitably accompanied by pressure. What if your daughter seems too busy or pressured? Perhaps she neglects practice, shows little interest in an activity, or says she wants to quit.

When evaluating whether your daughter should quit, consider her connectedness—if she's having fun and relating to peers—as much as her competence or skill level. Both connectedness and competence build self-confidence.

Tune into your daughter's cues. Listen when she talks about this activity and watch for signs that she's thriving: confidence, goal-setting, and exuberance. If you see those traits, you'll know that she is stretching but not overwhelmed—the perfect balance.

Dr. JoAnn Deak
Amy Lynch

TRY THIS

Do your best not to nag her about the activity in question. Instead, mention that you've noticed her interest seems to have declined. If things don't change within a couple of weeks, set a time to talk with her about this.

Observe her level of tiredness. Does she rebound from setbacks these days?

Consider the time remaining in the season or school term. Ask, "Can you push through for only (fill in the blank) more weeks?" Consider a break. Ask, "Would taking time off help you?"

Talk with her coach or instructor. Ask whether your daughter shows promise or interest. Extra encouragement from an instructor can make a difference.

If you and she decide to let an activity go, help her draft a note to her coach or instructor. Arranging her reasons on a page can help her solidify her decision, making it easier for her to explain it to her coach or instructor.

As parents, we often expect our children to do more and to do better than we did.

As your daughter grows older, grades begin to matter a lot more than before—to both of you.

While we may want our children to trump us academically, it's not their role to serve as extensions of our success. At the same time, it's reasonable to worry that without good grades, our daughters will not have opportunities to realize their full potential. How will you strike the parental balance that helps your daughter succeed in her own right? And what if academic success does not come easily for her?

As parents, we often get a powerful sense of gratification if our daughters bring home high grades; as long as she does that, we can assure ourselves that she's a good kid, a success. But what about a girl who's making C's or D's?

Remember that *relationship* comes first. Sure, there might be a C on that paper lying on the table, but you can make sure that it doesn't come between you.

Amy Lynch

TRY THIS

Don't compare her grades to your own at her age. School has changed so much that you'd be comparing apples to oranges. Instead, be genuinely curious. Ask, "How do you feel about this grade?" and really listen to her answers.

Look beyond the grade and ask the bigger questions that will really impact her future. Does she love to learn? Is she curious? Is she learning to listen, to reason, and to think for herself? These answers are key. If she's on a good track in these ways, the occasional low grade is a minor concern. If those things aren't true, it is time to work more closely with her teachers or to explore all the educational possibilities available to you and to her.

A girl's low grades in fifth or sixth grade may provide helpful clues about her learning style.

These are the years when your daughter's learning style is revealed. A low grade may throw a little fear into both of you, but use it as an opportunity to assess the way she learns best. What a joy to suddenly realize, "Ah, she really understands things you can count and measure. That's why she's good in science and less drawn to history."

Perhaps she has a keen sense of color but does not read quickly. Or maybe she plays piano with her eyes closed or picks up dance steps almost effortlessly. Or maybe she's great at playing memory games like Concentration.

During recent years, we've come to understand intelligence differently—as a wide and complex set of interrelated abilities unique to each individual. In fact, the types of intelligence measured by academic work are extremely limited. And when all is said and done, emotional and social intelligence may take a girl farther than pure academic ability. Help your daughter recognize and value her own particular intelligence and learning style.

Amy Lynch
Dr. JoAnn Deak

TRY THIS

Help your daughter notice and identify her learning strengths. Go to a restaurant together and eat your meal as you usually do. After leaving the restaurant, ask your daughter to describe the experience she just had. What types of things resonated most deeply for her? Sounds? Sights? Colors? Movement? Words? The "story" of the meal? The things she notices are clues to her learning style.

Go on a treasure hunt: discovering your daughter's strongest learning style is the treasure you seek. Research learning styles and types of intelligence online or at your daughter's school. Your daughter may not learn the same way you do. She may be a visual learner or an auditory one. Perhaps she learns best kinesthetically, through movement. Once you know the answers, you and her teachers can show her techniques that help her learn best.

Standing on Her Own Two Feet

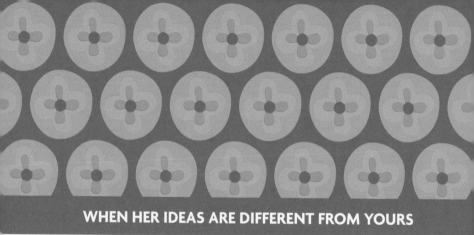

As your daughter goes through adolescence, she must formulate her own values, even when that means challenging your beliefs.

During these years, your daughter will struggle as never before with forming her identity and knowing herself. She will analyze her every tear, word, and thought, every detail of her body and appearance. Along with her own ruthless self-examination, she will question all that and more in her parents and friends.

As you gradually give your daughter more responsibility for thinking through problems and making her own decisions, she will sometimes voice values and ideas that are not the same as your own. Try not to dismiss her comments as a rebellion against you—they are an exploration of her heart. This process of questioning, examining, and testing beliefs and values is the only way she can make them her own.

Throughout this process, remember that you are—and will remain—your daughter's first teacher. Even as she questions them, the lessons you have instilled in her will continue to guide her.

Virginia Beane Rutter, MS

TRY THIS

Listen without interrupting. Remember that her talking about an idea does not mean she is going to act on that idea.

Ask questions in a nonjudgmental way. Try, "How did you come to this conclusion?"

If you disagree, respectfully acknowledge the differences in your beliefs. Try words such as, "I don't see it that way, but I understand that it makes sense to you," or "I respect your thinking on this issue. Here's what I believe . . . ," or "We are different people. We will always have differences of opinion."

Your daughter is acutely sensitive to discrepancies between what you say and what you do.

Your daughter sees whether or not you act on the beliefs you espouse. It's *you* she is watching as she hones her critical skills and forms her values. If she sees or hears you operating with double standards, she may be quick to point out your deceit.

Be honest with your daughter about your own behavior, and own up to your inconsistencies. And be gentle with yourself. Even the best parents have flaws! Remember that your overall example is more powerful than the occasional slip that you make.

Mom, as your daughter sees you and other adult women behave in strong, self-respecting ways, she will take those lessons to heart. Later, those lessons will resonate as part of her "inner voice," the force that guides her to know how to handle difficult decisions.

Dad, you play an equally crucial role, not only by supporting your daughter as she defines herself and acts on her beliefs, but also by showing her that you respect her mother and other women you know.

Virginia Beane Rutter, MS

TRY THIS

At the end of a day, try an "Oops" game: name a mistake you made during the day. Talk about how you made or will make things right. Let your daughter report any moments she wants to talk about.

If your daughter criticizes your failings, try words such as, "I wish I could always live up to my own ideals. I'm doing the best I can."

When she points out discrepancies in your behavior, try not to take her criticism personally. The very act of growing up and becoming more independent causes her to find fault with you. It's developmental, not personal. Do your best not to overreact. This phase really will pass. (Honest!)

No matter how young she is, your daughter grapples with ethical issues.

If your daughter is faced with a moral dilemma, such as seeing a classmate cheat on a test or making up her mind about a societal injustice, listen to her discomfort or outrage and help her sort out her options.

Encourage your daughter to list the actions she could take. Should she tell the teacher about the cheating? What are the ramifications if she does or doesn't? What is her responsibility to her class, to the community, and to herself? Probe her responses to help her think through the effects of the different options.

Virginia Beane Rutter, MS

TRY THIS

Ask, "Why is this upsetting? Why is this unfair?" When she voices her beliefs to you, she gains the confidence she needs to voice them to the world.

The image of a "decision tree" might help her sort through this problem. In this exercise, create the image of a tree in the air between you. Have her picture the problem based in the trunk of the tree. Each branch leading off from the trunk is a possible course of action, with several choices along the way. Help her explore each branch by asking, "And then what happens?" and "Who would be affected by that?"

Too much media exposure too soon not only confuses a girl, it wounds her spirit.

If we let them, news stories and so-called entertainment sources will drive explicit and violent images into our homes every day. Fortunately, when you protect your daughter from "adult" images and information, you give her time to develop her internal moral compass at a pace that is in sync with her age.

When your daughter is young, position yourself as her protector and ally against rough media. As she grows and wants to explore more, begin talking about the ways certain images and information are bad for our brains, our bodies, and our relationships.

Amy Lynch

TRY THIS

Pay attention to your gut instinct when deciding about particular television channels, movies, Web sites, books, and magazines. If you make decisions from that internal sense of what is healthy and what is not, your daughter will learn to do the same.

If your daughter objects when you prohibit something, talk about your feelings. Try, "That channel makes me feel angry," or "That Web site makes me feel icky and gross." After all, your feelings are your feelings. They may seem arbitrary to her, but they can't be argued away, not even by a masterful arguer like an 11-year-old girl!

Try saying, "I know we may renegotiate this in the future, but for now it's my job as a parent to say no."

If your daughter has been exposed to a violent video game or a movie that caused her distress, express your empathy for the hurt this experience can cause. Address the source if necessary: if she saw the offensive material in another family's home, you and she may want to talk about how she can respond if she wishes to visit the family again. Then she can say "no" firmly or use you as an excuse, as in, "My mom would ground me for a month if I watch that."

Let your daughter know that you are proud of her for developing the power to accept the things that are right for her and to recognize hurtful images and avoid them.

When you're having "big talks," express your values, but try not to use the discussion as a lecture platform. Remember that girls go deaf when we lecture more than we listen.

When you're discussing ethical or moral issues with your daughter, focus on eliciting her reaction to the situation instead of getting across your own point of view. You'll be helping her practice defining herself in matters of importance, and your respect for her opinions will strengthen your relationship.

Weave issue-based talks into your family life. At the dinner table or when driving your daughter to activities, start discussions about environmental issues, animal rights, local news, politics, and other social concerns. This kind of dialogue sharpens her thinking skills and expands her awareness of larger issues.

Virginia Beane Rutter, MS

TRY THIS

Give yourself "parent points" each time you forego a lecture and, instead, ask your daughter, "What do you think about that?" Practice listening—really listening—as she explores all kinds of issues. And be sure you have adult outlets to explore your own views thoroughly, so that you don't feel squelched.

Look for little things—trash on the ground, stories in the newspaper, magazine covers, billboards, or election signs—and ask your daughter what she thinks about what's going on. Sometimes, the more you ask, the more she learns.

For your daughter to have integrity, she has to acknowledge all of her feelings, not just the socially acceptable ones.

As parents, we are role models for how to make room for our negative feelings without using them to hurt other people. It is from you that your daughter learns to be her own person by speaking the truth, even if that makes other people unhappy.

Encourage your daughter to be "emotionally real" with herself and others; she doesn't always have to be sweet and nice. This means that when she begins to withdraw or be angry with you, you will understand that she has the right to her own feelings.

Talk about her feelings and yours, and resolve conflicts in healthy ways that reconnect you after a blowup. Likewise, if you see your daughter fly into a rage at her brother or a friend, teach her to communicate her displeasure in other ways. Show her that working through the shadowy side of life is just as important and productive as celebrating the happy side.

Virginia Beane Rutter, MS

TRY THIS

If your daughter has strong feelings but finds it hard to talk about them, mirror what you see in her without embarrassing her. Say matter-of-factly, "I see you aren't smiling today," or "I heard your door slam. Is there anything I can do?" If she shakes her head "no," suggest that she write about what she is feeling.

This is a good time to give her a journal in which she can record her deepest secrets, including those feelings that she hesitates to share. Tell her that, often, feelings sort themselves out and become clearer if she can get them on paper, and tell her that she may want to talk about them later. If she does blurt something out, don't try to talk her out of her feelings. Keep asking questions to help her understand herself, or just let her have a good cry.

Share some of your own painful feelings with her in appropriate ways. If you are upset, angry, or sad, let her know. Stress the difference between talking about feelings and using them to hurt others.

If you and she are in conflict, acknowledge her feelings. Take breaks in the conversation. This teaches her how to manage her emotions.

A tween girl needs two conflicting things at once: to make up her own mind and to be part of a group.

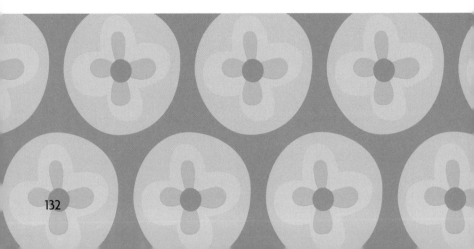

There is often a conflict between a girl's individual wishes and her desire to go along with everything her peers believe, think, and want her to do in order to join their "club."

At the same time, she is also learning from her peers in healthy ways. You can help your daughter walk the fine line between her individuality and relating to her friends.

Virginia Beane Rutter, MS

TRY THIS

Use the analogy of a path. On a sheet of paper, ask her to draw a "path"—the path to her grown-up self. Where is she on the path *now*? What comes next, and what's after that? Use this time to dream big. Where will the path of her life go? What exciting things might she find along the way?

When she has finished, point out that her friends have paths, too. At times her path will overlap with theirs, but at other times they will lead in different directions. Tell her a story about how your path diverged from a girlfriend's.

If you notice your daughter going along with the crowd too frequently, evaluate the situation discreetly from a distance. Ask her how she feels about doing what her friends want her to do. If she is open to your input, offer gentle suggestions as to how she might change her behavior. Say, for example, "Next time, why don't you say, 'Last time we saw the movie you wanted to see. This time I'd really like to choose.' "

As active and busy as her life may be, your daughter also needs solitude.

For a girl your daughter's age, time alone can become sacred. The more self-reflection your daughter fosters, the more she will know herself and be true to herself when it comes to working toward her own goals.

If your daughter is grounded in her own thoughts, feelings, and imagination, she will be less susceptible to peer pressure. Whether she retreats to her room or to a favorite spot in nature—a creek or a park—she can feel her own wholeness. Once she has learned this skill, she will be able to renew herself whenever she feels depleted.

Virginia Beane Rutter, MS

TRY THIS

Suggest that your daughter keep a time diary for a few days. How many hours does she spend reading, eating meals, in class, and socializing? Create your own diary and compare notes. Ask, "Did either of us have the time we needed to relax and daydream? Did we spend enough time outdoors?"

Open her eyes to good books with female heroines. Give her time to herself to reflect, read, and dream. Just as you find good books for your daughter, ask her to recommend good books to you. You'll find lots to talk about, including the ways the heroines spent time alone to build their strength and character.

Our daughters' generation is more diverse and inclusive than any in history. Yet tensions remain. Your attitude makes a difference.

Many girls today routinely travel to other countries and find friends with similar interests around the globe. Technology makes it easier for our daughters to learn about and feel part of other cultures. But a small world is not the same as a friendly one. Our daughters have grown up during a time of international tension.

If ethnic tensions surface in your daughter's school or in your community, speak about that with her. Express your faith that most people want peace and that there are good people in every group.

Do all you can to give your daughter travel opportunities. The more she knows about the world, the more she will be able to manage its challenges and become what demographers call a *thrival*—someone who is at home in many cultures.

Amy Lynch

TRY THIS

The next time you take a family trip, have a contest to see who hears the most languages during the course of the trip. (Extra points for having the courage to ask what language it is you're hearing!)

Ask your daughter what she knows about various groups of people. Her breadth of knowledge may surprise you.

Help her learn even more about other cultures in fun ways. If your daughter wants to go out to dinner, take her to an ethnic restaurant where she can try a new cuisine.

Talk to your daughter about the various groups in her own family history and the struggles they faced.

Girls who know where they came from become more certain about where they're going.

Whatever your roots—or hers—use family stories or cultural celebrations to teach your daughter to appreciate her family background. This knowledge will make her feel grounded and strong and help her better understand herself.

Virginia Beane Rutter, MS

TRY THIS

Go through old family photo albums with your daughter, and share stories about the people and characters within their pages. Teach her a family recipe and share your memories of eating that dish as a child. Make a scrapbook together using copies of her favorite family photos. Make a family tree as a craft project.

Show your daughter your baby book. Tween girls love hearing what their parents were like as children; set your daughter up with a grandparent or older relative and let them dish about you—the good, the bad, and the funny.

Don't forget music and art! Go online or to your local music store and find traditional music from your ancestors' native lands (or from hers, if your daughter's ethnic heritage differs from your own). Play these recordings during dinner. What kinds of art come from the countries of her ancestors? What does this art tell her and you about the people themselves?

A girl who has been raised with the idea that together we can make a difference most assuredly will.

What parent does not want to raise a child who recognizes the needs of others and is grateful for what she has?

When you weave the spirit of giving into the fabric of your family's identity, the rewards are immeasurable. You instill in your daughter a sense of empathy and self-worth. You create opportunities to bond with your daughter and to tell her how proud you are of her abilities and her warm, giving heart. And you show your daughter how she can affect others' lives.

Patti Kelley Criswell, MSW

TRY THIS

Share your concern about other people with comments such as, "We need to think of Mrs. Wilson today. She's having surgery." Giving your daughter a chance to act—for example, sending a get-well note to Mrs. Wilson—helps her feel that she is part of the larger community.

Limit the time she spends watching TV characters and reality-show participants who display hateful attitudes or a lack of empathy. Conversely, comment on acts of kindness you see. Reading aloud an article from the paper about a selfless hero shows your daughter that you respect that kind of behavior.

Make shopping for those less fortunate an annual tradition each holiday season. The acts of kindness you involve your daughter in while she's young will likely become second nature for her later on.

Teach your daughter to keep a balance of power in any friendship—whether it's with a boy or a girl.

S tudies show that girls give in to risky behaviors (such as smoking or early sexual activity) not so much in response to direct pressure but in order to fit in and stay on good terms with people they care about. It may be hard for your daughter to say no because she doesn't want to hurt someone's feelings or be outside the group.

She should never hesitate to say no to anyone—boy or girl—because she is afraid of hurting his feelings or embarrassing him, or because she thinks that person has a right to be aggressive.

Dr. Lynn Ponton

TRY THIS

If you suspect your daughter is saying yes when she should be saying no, talk about it with her. You might start by asking about other kids, as in, "Do you think Jenny feels like she has to smoke?" Or, "What about the kids from youth group? Do people kiss or do they do more?" This lets you state your expectations and your worries without accusing her of something.

If you need to address her behavior, you may want to start with, "I know you feel close to (fill in the blank with the friend or friends with whom she shares the behavior)." This acknowledges her good heart and connection with her friends and makes it easier for her to hear what you're going to say next.

Tell her that "yes" and "no" are not a game. Try, "You need to tell people no when you mean no and yes when you mean yes. And let them know you mean what you say." There should be no gray area here.

If you are willing to discuss the appeals of risky behaviors, you can build bridges instead of walls when you talk with your daughter about these subjects.

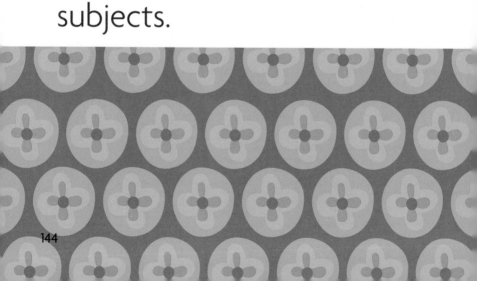

During the elementary school years, girls learn that smoking is harmful. But when girls enter middle school, cigarettes become more alluring for their so-called "coolness factor." And despite some backlash, smoking and drinking are still made to look inviting in media images designed to reach our daughters.

It can be helpful to acknowledge that smoking has always looked cool to young people, maybe even to you when you were young. Acknowledging what is alluring or attractive about risky behaviors can open the door to a conversation about "perception versus reality."

Dr. Lynn Ponton

TRY THIS

If you find yourself watching a movie with your daughter in which young people smoke, drink, or use illicit substances, use the opportunity to talk. Help her look beyond the surface and recognize the dangers that are portrayed. When you see young actresses smoking or drinking on television, talk with your daughter about the situations shown.

Resist lecturing. Ask your daughter questions instead. Does the ad or program make it seem as if the risky behavior will solve the girl's problem, make her feel better, or make her more popular? Does the program portray stereotypical behavior—is it the "bad girl" or "cool girl" who smokes? Could that character really lead the exciting, active lifestyle shown if she were a chronic smoker or drinker? Help your daughter see the hidden risks behind the behavior.

Talk about the immediate consequences of the behaviors. Getting cancer usually seems pretty distant to a girl of twelve, but "yellow teeth" and "bad breath" will get her attention right away.

How will you know if your daughter is really ready to stay home alone, and how will you keep her safe if she is?

Your daughter's attitude is the most important indicator of readiness for staying alone. Does she seem calm and self-assured about the idea of being home independently? Does a brief time on her own feel like a natural phase in her growing independence rather than an abrupt change? Does she follow rules responsibly and remember instructions you give her?

Probe your own feelings. Do you feel confident she can handle everyday situations? If so, start the conversation with her by generating a list of safety rules for staying home alone.

Amy Lynch

TRY THIS

Write down firm dos and don'ts so that you can be very clear about them with your daughter. Ask "what if" questions: for example, "What if someone rings the doorbell?" or "What if you get a phone call or an e-mail from someone you don't know?" Brainstorm answers together.

Specify how your daughter can use her time alone—for example, on art projects, chores, phone calls, or reading. Determine which appliances she can use in your absence. Decide whom she is to call in case of emergency. Set clear boundaries about acceptable TV and computer use. Set up a schedule for regular check-in calls with you.

Researchers find that girls left on their own for more than ten hours a week feel the stress of loneliness.

A girl of ten or twelve needs time on her own, but she needs connection, too. The hours she spends alone must be limited.

Researchers find that girls who spend more than ten hours a week alone have a higher risk of becoming despondent or depressed, and they are more vulnerable to breaking the rules you've set about visitors, Internet use, TV, or going outside.

Amy Lynch

TRY THIS

Go to your local library, bookstore, craft shop, and toy store. Stock up on interesting books, easy craft kits, and puzzles. Ask your daughter to designate a special place for her "home-alone surprises." Each time you leave her alone, leave a surprise in that special place. Tell her to call you or send a text message about the item you left for her.

If your daughter will be home alone regularly, program in healthy connections such as phone calls to relatives.

When you get home, tune in and listen carefully. Ask about everything—her conversations with friends, the books she read, her on-line time, and the shows she watched on TV. If you hear the distinct note of pride or self-assurance in her voice, then you'll know that her time alone was spent in the best of company.

Reaching for the Stars

To your daughter, life's possibilities can appear infinite.

Your daughter's curiosity and energy may seem boundless to you. Like a sponge, she soaks up whatever ideas intrigue her. That's why it's important to give her as many enriching experiences as possible and to expose her to experts in diverse fields.

As she pursues her interests, your daughter gains much in the process. Sorting through her own experiences and preferences gives her crucial information about herself. She discovers that some interests are temporary diversions and that other causes are things she believes in with all her heart.

You probably have strong opinions about her future, too, and your ideas have been shaped by your own triumphs and disappointments. But give your daughter a chance to draw her own conclusions and make her own choices. The more she is encouraged to use her genuine feelings as her guide, the better she will come to know and trust herself.

Dr. Roni Cohen-Sandler

TRY THIS

Listen for clues about what subjects your daughter likes and is drawn to. Channel her curiosity by exposing her to experiences that build on her interests. You might visit historical sites, museums, or Web sites that you have scouted out beforehand.

Best of all, use your network of friends and colleagues to introduce your daughter to people working in her fields of interest. She might strike up a conversation or an e-mail exchange with a professor, a scientist, an anthropologist, or an artisan who encourages her to dream big.

Nothing is more empowering than conveying, "I believe in you."

Regardless of our backgrounds, the greatest gift we can give our girls is simple: taking our daughters seriously and believing in their dreams.

Your support should not be confined merely to your words. Consider what the everyday tasks you do for your daughter communicate about your attitude.

Dr. Roni Cohen-Sandler

TRY THIS

Think about the message you send your daughter as you support—or don't support—her in her activities. Everyday things matter. Do you drive her cheerfully to her practices, lessons, and games and pick her up on time? Do you keep track of her schedule and attend her events? What does your daughter hear you say about her dreams as you speak with others?

Think, too, about how you conduct your own life. How do you handle being harried or feeling overwhelmed by responsibilities? How do you cope with the sting of failure? Do you handle disappointment with grace?

It may be daunting to consider the many daily opportunities you have to model stamina, flexibility, and determination. But when you demonstrate these qualities, be assured your daughter is watching closely and appreciatively.

Girls have powerful radar. They know whether we think their goals are foolish or really can be achieved.

In spite of their bravado, girls usually look to adults for validation and confirmation. So when our daughters entrust us with their deepest dreams, they feel vulnerable and may be on the lookout for even the subtlest of reactions.

Your emotions and relationship with your daughter influence her dreams enormously. If some of her aspirations give you pause, keep your anxiety in check. If you are unduly hesitant when she talks with you about them, she may second-guess her goals. But if you believe, she will have the courage to work toward her dreams.

Dr. Roni Cohen-Sandler

TRY THIS

Find some time to reflect on your own ambitions as a ten-year-old. That's a pivotal year for many of us, a time when we have big dreams yet also begin thinking in mature ways. What happened when you were ten, eleven, or twelve years old that helped you feel you could make things happen in the world? What happened that discouraged you? This is insight you can use as you guide your daughter through her tween years.

During childhood, your daughter's dreams may be so big that they're not realistic. For now, that's O.K.

Regardless of your daughter's age or the grandeur of her ideas, listen carefully to find out what interests her. When in elementary school, she may want to be a skydiver, a scientist, a mom, and a fashion designer—all at once! At this age, it's O.K. if her goals are sky-high and impractical.

Hold off on throwing cold water on your daughter's ambitions. If she sings off-key, she may not be Broadway bound (as she now hopes), but the church choir will welcome her. You don't have to share all your years of wisdom about life in the real world just yet. She has plenty of time from middle school on up to be concerned about her own limitations and the obstacles to realizing her dreams.

Dr. Roni Cohen-Sandler

TRY THIS

When she proposes a future that is beyond anything that you know to be possible, try saying something like, "Wow, great ideas! You will have a fascinating life."

When she hits fifth or sixth grade, go the next step by saying, "Of course you can do all those things, but you may need to do them one at a time, or only a couple at a time."

By the time she's in middle school, she'll understand more about the actual number of hours in the day and naturally start to focus her energies on which of her goals she'll achieve first.

What do you do if your daughter idolizes a teenage actress or pop singer whose behavior you consider inappropriate?

It helps to remember what matters most to girls of this age. Fitting in means everything; if your daughter's friends are excited about the latest teen singer or actress, it's likely she will be, too.

During her tweens and teens, your daughter is beginning to figure out what womanhood is all about. Hollywood is brilliant at packaging glitzy starlets who appeal to youngsters; unfortunately, these icons are often associated with messages and images that degrade females. With your help, your daughter can become a good judge of character and a pretty sophisticated social critic.

Dr. Evelyn Bassoff

TRY THIS

Engage your daughter in a conversation about her favorite musical artists. Listen respectfully to what she has to say, and share your opinions respectfully. She may not react overtly, but she will take your opinions to heart.

You might say, "I agree with you that _____ is pretty and talented, but it bothers me that she shows off her body to get attention." Ask your daughter how she feels about this. Such a talk may help her begin to question the role of women as sex objects. It may also help her see that it's possible to admire someone's talents and at the same time recognize his or her faults.

Point out behind-the-scenes roles that your daughter might not know about. Teach her that she can choose to be a performer or someone who creates art—the movie director, the choreographer, or the songwriter.

Try to expand your daughter's role models beyond pop stars. Talk to her about female artists, musicians, authors, scientists, athletes, and world leaders. Take every opportunity that comes your way to introduce her to real women who do interesting things.

Even if your daughter's goals have seemingly low odds for success, talk with her about how she could achieve them.

Your daughter needs practical guidance. You can help her connect what she is doing now—her education, practice, and training—with her future goals.

Whether or not you think her current goal will "stick," you are the person who can help your daughter see how her dreams can become reality.

Dr. Roni Cohen-Sandler

TRY THIS

Help your daughter break down her goals into achievable steps. Put her goal at the top of a page or chart, and then list below that goal the steps she would take to get there. Work from the future (the goal she wants to achieve) backward to the present.

For example, a page might read "Goal: Fashion Designer" at the top. Below that, working from top to bottom, you and she might write:

• Study design in art school or college.

• Do summer internships with designers and tailors.

• Take high school art classes and classes in color and textiles at a local art school.

• Work part-time in a store that sells interesting clothing.

• Take a trip to see a historical fashion exhibit at the Smithsonian.

• Locate a designer in a nearby city. Call and ask to interview her.

• Take a sewing class at the YWCA.

• Download online images and make an inspirational fashion board for my room.

Girls are motivated to make the world a better, fairer place.

Many girls are energized not only by the thought of achieving their own goals but also by correcting inequalities in the world around them. When your daughter is impassioned by a cause—whether it's animal rights, the environment, or a lack of good lunch options in the school cafeteria—you can help her feel empowered.

It's normal, however, for you to have mixed feelings about this. You may find her concerns admirable, yet you want to protect her from the trials involved in making groundbreaking changes in society.

Dr. Roni Cohen-Sandler

TRY THIS

Anticipate the obstacles your daughter may face. Discuss with her how novel and untested ideas are sometimes distrusted and how successful pioneers persevered to overcome roadblocks.

Assure her that, even if she doesn't make things change as much as she would like, "Every little bit counts. Your voice matters. You never know how much impact you have."

When necessary, allow her to fail. Failure is a necessary experience. It helps your daughter shift her priorities and adjust her goals. Point out the skills she has learned from circulating a petition, e-mailing lawmakers, or organizing others to help. Assure her that her efforts are never wasted, that people heard her message and will make more change next time.

Have you identified the boundaries between your daughter's ambitions and your ambitions for her?

Your ability to support your daughter in reaching her goals speaks volumes. Acknowledging your daughter as a separate individual with her own valid goals helps her develop a strong sense of who she is and who she wants to become.

As she matures, your daughter should increasingly rely on her own feelings to learn what intrigues her. The more she is permitted to stay in touch with her inner life rather than having to please others—yes, including us parents—the more satisfied and fulfilled she will ultimately become.

If you often feel conflicted or angry about your daughter's interests or activities, this may be a sign that you have not defined the boundaries between your daughter's identity and your own. This is an understandable confusion. Yet, in the short run it can cause a girl to feel that "Mom doesn't understand me." In the long run, it can bring about years of pain and misunderstanding.

Dr. Roni Cohen-Sandler

TRY THIS

If your mother is available, ask her about the dreams she had as a girl. What did she aspire to? Now recall your own dreams. Remember how strongly you knew that you had to separate from your mother and follow your own path? Reflect on how much things have changed between your generation and your daughter's. Given all that change, her dreams are naturally different from your own.

Look for these signals that you are confusing your daughter's dreams with your own:

• The same conflicts about her interests come up again and again.
• You see your daughter differently than other people see her. For example, you see her as outgoing while others see her as shy.
• Your daughter often tells you that what you say about her doesn't make sense or doesn't pertain to her.

If your past comes up in conversation when you're talking with your daughter about her ambitions, try adding, "That was my experience, but it may not be yours."

Nothing is more painful than watching your daughter's heart break.

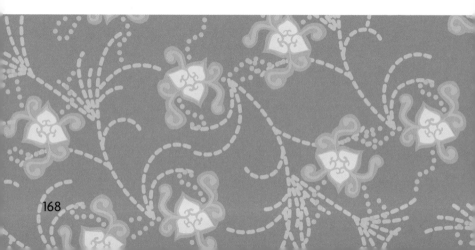

When your daughter dares to hope, there is, of course, the chance that those hopes will be dashed: she won't make the team or get the grade she wanted. When disappointment comes, your daughter may respond by being sad, furious, or even vengeful. All these feelings are normal reactions to hurt and loss.

The most helpful thing a parent can do is guide a daughter to be realistic about her skills and not label herself negatively. She is not "the worst person on the planet" or "hated by everyone." Rather than allowing her to focus on qualities she thinks she lacks or people she might want to blame, help her identify things she couldn't control or might want to do differently next time.

The most successful individuals are the hopeful ones: the people who reach for goals that are attainable but also require effort, who find ways around obstacles and keep trying.

Dr. Roni Cohen-Sandler
Dr. Lynda Madison

TRY THIS

You cannot assure your daughter that life will be fair, but you can help her handle whatever happens. If she comes home distraught, listen to her and let her cry if she feels like it. Tell her that you can see she is hurting and that you're sorry things turned out this way.

As you console your daughter, let her know you are impressed with her gutsiness in going for goals, not just with her successes.

After she has had a few days to digest her disappointment, try this Giant Step game (similar to Mother, May I?). Find a time when she is hanging out watching you do something such as stirring a pot of spaghetti sauce in the kitchen. Ask her to stand against a wall facing you. Suggest she take one giant step forward each time she can say something she does well. You can chime in, too, with successes she may have forgotten. Keep it silly and have her move all over the kitchen. Here's the best part: at the finish she ends up with a big hug from you.

When your daughter is disappointed, she may decide to try harder next time—or to never try again.

When your daughter doesn't succeed at an endeavor, rather than allowing her to decide that she is a bad or untalented person, help her to attribute the loss or failure to situational factors that she might be able to fix—by preparing differently, not being overtired, or having fewer things to do. You can also help her find talents that are her real forte.

Dr. Lynda Madison

TRY THIS

Try to understand and empathize with her feelings. Talk with her about whether she might ever go after this goal again and what she would do differently if she did. Ask her how she thinks you could help.

Girls with resilience have learned to think three things when they fail:

1. "This failure is not my whole life. There are parts of my life that are not affected by this."
2. "I will not always feel this way. Tomorrow morning (or next week) I will feel better. I won't let how I feel now stop me from trying again."
3. "This is not entirely my fault. There are factors involved that I cannot control."

Plant these three ideas among her thoughts each time she fails, and you'll build her ability to bounce back from disappointment.

We parent best when we think of ourselves as privileged to observe rather than needing to control.

We are always saying good-bye to the girls we love—good-bye to the precious infants they were and to the charming toddlers and energetic preschoolers we once knew. Those good-byes don't slow down during the tween years. The girls we knew and loved a year ago kept changing as we watched.

Each day our daughters are becoming. Our role—and it is a sacred one—is to guide, observe, and celebrate.

Amy Lynch

TRY THIS

If your daughter seems uncertain or is going through a rocky time, do a "These true things" ritual. If she is nine years old, help her write down nine true things about herself. If she is eight, it's eight true things, or twelve true things if she is twelve.

Anytime you can make the experience physical, the lesson will resonate even more with your daughter and remain in her memory bank longer. So, after having her make a list, let her choose strands of embroidery floss in a different color for each "true thing." Have her braid the floss into a bracelet that she can wear to remember the unique person she is becoming.

Help your daughter help herself with advice books from American Girl, written specifically for girls ages 8 to 12. These books will give her the tools and confidence she needs to make smart, healthy decisions for herself and her body.

The Care & Keeping of You: The Body Book for Girls

This bestseller offers girls practical, age-appropriate information about everything from hair care and healthy eating to periods and pimples. *The Care & Keeping of You Journal* helps girls stay in touch with their changing bodies.

"Thanks for the book The Care & Keeping of You. *After I read it, I felt like I could tell my mom anything, anytime, anywhere."*
—An American girl

The Feelings Book: The Care & Keeping of Your Emotions

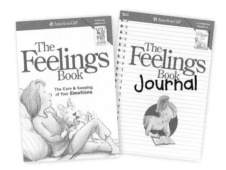

This book gives girls straightforward advice on how to handle all kinds of emotions and how to get help when they really need it. *The Feelings Book Journal* uses quizzes, fill-in-the-blanks, and checklists to offer girls more practice in dealing with difficult feelings.

American Girl created **Smart Girl's Guides** to address the topics that girls worry about most, such as troubles with friends, starting middle school, and dealing with divorce. Each book uses quizzes, real-life scenarios, and letters and tips from other girls to deliver sound advice in a friendly, easily digestible way.

For more information and to see American Girl's full line of advice books, visit your local bookstore or **americangirl.com**.

Published by American Girl Publishing, Inc.
Copyright © 2009 by American Girl, LLC

All rights reserved. No part of this book may be used or reproduced in
any manner whatsoever without written permission except in the case
of brief quotations embodied in critical articles and reviews.

Questions or comments? Call 1-800-845-0005,
visit our Web site at **americangirl.com**,
or write to Customer Service, American Girl,
8400 Fairway Place, Middleton, WI 53562-0497.

Printed in China
10 11 12 13 14 15 LEO 10 9 8 7 6 5 4 3

All American Girl marks are trademarks of American Girl, LLC.

Editorial development: Therese Kauchak Maring, Michelle Nowadly Watkins, Erin Falligant
Design: Chris Lorette David
Production: Judith Lary, Jeannette Bailey, Kendra Schluter, Tami Kepler
Special thanks: Vivian Slade

This book is not intended to replace the advice of or treatment by physicians, psychologists, or
other experts. It should be considered an additional resource only. Questions and concerns about
mental or physical health should always be discussed with a doctor or other health-care provider.

Portions of the advice in this book first appeared in *What I Wish You Knew*,
published by American Girl, and on **americangirl.com.**

Very special thanks to
Therese Maring and Michelle Watkins,
who truly know how to listen to girls

Library of Congress Cataloging-in-Publication Data

Raising an American girl : parenting advice for the real world.

p. cm.

ISBN 978-1-59369-618-4

1. Girls—United States. 2. Parenting—United States. 3. Child rearing—United States.

I. American Girl (Firm).

HQ777. R26 2009   649'.1330973—dc22   2009029955

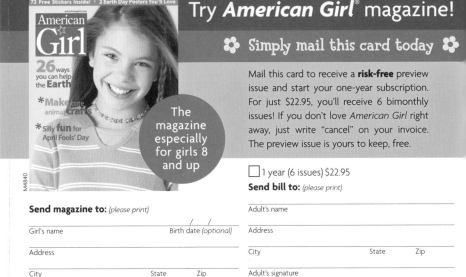

72 Free Stickers Inside! ✻ 2 Earth Day Posters You'll Love

Try *American Girl*® magazine!

✿ Simply mail this card today ✿

American Girl

26 ways you can help the Earth

* Make cute animal crafts
* Silly fun for April Fools' Day

The magazine especially for girls 8 and up

M4840

Mail this card to receive a **risk-free** preview issue and start your one-year subscription. For just $22.95, you'll receive 6 bimonthly issues! If you don't love *American Girl* right away, just write "cancel" on your invoice. The preview issue is yours to keep, free.

☐ 1 year (6 issues) $22.95
Send bill to: *(please print)*

Send magazine to: *(please print)*

Girl's name   Birth date *(optional)*

Address

City   State   Zip

Adult's name

Address

City   State   Zip

Adult's signature

Guarantee: You may cancel at any time and receive a full refund on all unserved issues. Allow 4-6 weeks for first issue. Non-US subscriptions $29 US, prepaid only. To learn more about *American Girl* magazine or remove your name from our mailing list, please call 800-234-1278. © 2010 American Girl, LLC.

K01AGL

Request a FREE catalogue!

Books are just the beginning...

Discover dolls, clothing, furniture, and accessories that inspire girls to imagine their own stories.

Just mail this card, call 1-800-845-0005, or visit americangirl.com.

Parent's name   Girl's birth date

Address

City   State   Zip

Parent's e-mail *(provide to receive updates and Web-exclusive offers)*

(   )
Parent's phone   ☐ Home ☐ Work

Parent's signature   12583i

Send a catalogue to a grandparent or a friend:

Name

Address

City   State   Zip

☐ Grandparent 152621i   ☐ Friend 12591i

Today's date

C3320

NO POSTAGE
NECESSARY
IF MAILED
IN THE
UNITED STATES

BUSINESS REPLY MAIL

FIRST-CLASS MAIL   PERMIT NO. 190   BOONE IA

POSTAGE WILL BE PAID BY ADDRESSEE

 American Girl®
Magazine Subscription Dept.
PO BOX 5532
HARLAN IA 51593-3032

Visit americangirl.com
and click on **Fun for Girls**
for quizzes and games.

Place
Stamp
Here

 American Girl®
PO BOX 620497
MIDDLETON WI 53562-0497